PENGUIN BOOKS
ALMOST HUMAN

Barbara Woodhouse was born in Rathfarnham, County Dublin, in 1910. After the death of her father when she was nine, the family moved to Brighton, and later to Oxford. She was educated at Headington School for Girls and then at Harper Adams Agricultural College, Newport, Shropshire. She lived in the Argentine from 1934 to 1937, and on her return to England went to live again in Oxford, where she married Dr Michael Woodhouse. For twenty-one years she ran a farm, bred Arabs, broke in horses and trained dogs.

Barbara Woodhouse shot to fame with her television series 'Train Your Dog the Woodhouse Way' and in 1980 she was named Female Television Personality of the Year by Pye in association with the Writers' Guild of Great Britain. She has made six films for cinema release, including *Along the Way*. Her dogs Juno and Junia made over a hundred film and television appearances. Her other publications include *Dog Training My Way*, *No Bad Dogs*, *A–Z of Dogs and Puppies*, *Talking to Animals* (Penguin) and *Just Barbara*; she has recently made an LP, *Training Dogs Her Way*.

Almost Human

BARBARA WOODHOUSE

PENGUIN BOOKS

Penguin Books Ltd, Harmondsworth, Middlesex, England
Penguin Books, 625 Madison Avenue, New York, New York 10022, U.S.A.
Penguin Books Australia Ltd, Ringwood, Victoria, Australia
Penguin Books Canada Ltd, 2801 John Street, Markham, Ontario, Canada L3R 1B4
Penguin Books (N.Z.) Ltd, 182–190 Wairau Road, Auckland 10, New Zealand

First published by Barbara Woodhouse, 1976
Published by Allen Lane 1981
Published in Penguin Books 1981

Made and printed in Great Britain by
Richard Clay (The Chaucer Press) Ltd, Bungay, Suffolk
Set in Monophoto Ehrhardt

Contents

Acknowledgements

My most grateful thanks to everyone who has helped me with this book, especially John D. Drysdale for permission to include some of his superb photographs; the *Daily Mirror*; the Children's Film Foundation; *Radio Times*; and Mr Thompson of Sun Photographic Bureau Ltd.

To Keith Dorken of Hazell Watson & Viney for all his help and guidance.

Preface

In writing this book about my life with my Great
Danes, I have tried to tell my readers just how human
these dogs can be. I am sure I never had an inkling
when I had my first Dane that I should ever own dogs
that became film stars and television personalities. It
was only when I realized what great intelligence can be
nurtured in these dogs that I wanted to develop their
brains and personalities so that they could live up to
the words so often heard from owners of all breeds
that their dogs are 'almost human'.

My Danes were treated in exactly the same way as
our children, and in so doing I learnt an awful lot
about how much dogs like to be included in everything
the family does. I am sure not many people would
think of allowing their dogs to hoover the carpets, or
water the garden, or ring the gong for meals, yet these
were three of the many things my Danes liked doing.

By the end of their lives I am sure they knew at least 250 words and their meaning.

I hope people will find this a helpful autobiography, for I have included some advice to try and help owners of these beautiful dogs, in fact all dogs who have somewhat similar needs.

The great tragedy of unwanted Great Danes who grow too big for people who have bought them, or eat too much, or who don't behave as they should distresses me deeply. I hope therefore this book may open the eyes of owners, or would-be owners, before they take into their homes these wonderful dogs, who give so much and ask so little in return.

Some time ago I was talking to a Dane owner who asked my advice before buying a Dane, and then did exactly the opposite to what I had advised. Some nine months later he kept me three-quarters of an hour on the telephone in utter despair telling me the dog was now going for other dogs, had developed a guarding instinct when it was near his wife and was inclined to go for people, and that he bought it with the understanding that the breeder could use it for stud purposes. This last contract was in my opinion a quite stupid way to own a pet dog, for make no mistake, having a stud dog is not the best way to own any dog. That should be left to breeders. The puppy had not been trained at three months to leave other dogs alone, nor to be friendly on command to strangers. It was not even clean in the house. You can't blame the dog for any of these faults. I am perfectly certain that, had he done what I told him to do, that puppy could have grown up just as well adjusted, intelligent and wonderful to own as most Great Danes are. The poor things don't choose their owners, they have to put up with them. If the dog turns out badly, the breed gets a bad name. Few people lay the blame on the owner.

I had a letter recently from someone contemplating her first Dane; she asked, would it matter if she left it alone all day three days a week as she wanted to keep on working that time? My reply was, how could you contemplate solitary confinement for a dog three days a week? How could it be clean, or happy, under these circumstances? I shan't hear any more until she goes ahead with exactly what she intended doing in the first place, giving another dog a horrible life, and gets possibly a not very nice dog as a result.

To all Dane owners who have lovely happy dogs treated as Danes should be treated, I say 'You lucky people'.

A Dane puppy's plea to its owner

With every bark and loving sign
Let me be yours, and you be mine.
Love me, train me, let me be
Your closest friend eternally.

I

Jean, My First Dane

Jean's life had only twenty hours to go when chance led me to meet her. I was staying with an old Oxford friend of mine at Hartburn near Stockton-on-Tees and he was invited round to drinks with some neighbours. When we arrived there I saw this huge Great Dane lying on a sofa and went over to talk to her. She instantly snuggled up to me and I asked how old she was and they told me six years old, but the sad thing was she was going to be put to sleep in the morning as her owners couldn't keep her. The present people she was with already had two other dogs and really couldn't have a Great Dane. Instantly I said, 'Could I have her?' and of course they were utterly delighted.

Next morning I set off for my home at Oxford in my small Wolseley Daytona sports car with the passenger seat taken out so that Jean could lie down beside me for the journey of 200 miles. Jean had obviously belonged to someone who was a fast driver. In those early days of motoring there were very few cars on the road, no speed limits to worry about and my bright green car suited her taste in motoring. Every time I slowed down she sat up to see why on earth I'd done such a thing, then, satisfied there was no hold up, would settle down at once for a further sleep.

We arrived at my home in Oxford and I took her straight indoors to Mother. I'd expected her to welcome Jean with open arms, but she hesitated because Jean certainly smelt. I don't think she'd had a bath for years, and Mother's first reaction was to hold her nose and say, 'Barbara, you can't have that dog indoors, she stinks. She'll have to go out in a stable.' I think this was the first time in my life I'd ever not done what my Mother told me to do, for we were brought up to be obedient, but Jean was not going out into a loose box and I said so. I said I'd bath her and she could live in my bedroom. I never quite understood my Mother's attitude towards animals in the house. Our Alsatian and Fox Terrier always slept in the stable and were never allowed in the house under any circumstances. For someone as fond of animals as my Mother was, I never understood why our home couldn't have the dogs in it too.

Jean never left me. I bought her a huge emerald green patent collar which matched my green car and also my best suit which I wore when going places.

Jean stopped everyone who passed her, they just had to pat her. I reckon anyone without friends could easily make them with a Great Dane.

I had only had Jean about six months when I

accepted an invitation to go out to the Argentine to friends, my obsession being horses, and the thought of living with 6,000 horses on the *estancia* I'd been invited to whetted my appetite for the wide open spaces. Mother said she would look after Jean until I found out whether the country was suitable for a big dog. When I discovered that dogs were at home there even though the heat was quite intense in summer, I asked Mother to ship Jean out to me. She came on a Royal Mail boat which took a month to reach Buenos Aires and on the journey she got kicked by a drunken sailor, so a passenger told me, and had a nasty lump on her back leg which left her with a slight limp. When I saw the boat coming in to dock I could see Jean being held by a lady and I did a silly thing, I whistled her. She went nearly mad, but luckily didn't do anything dangerous. I just couldn't wait to see if she remembered me. We spent the night in an hotel in Buenos Aires and then took the train up to Entre Rios and the *estancia*. The Indian employees were struck dumb when they saw this enormous dog, they'd never seen anything bigger than the *estancia* pointer.

Jean soon settled down and went out every day riding with me in the camp for miles and miles. I taught her to find the baby lambs that had fallen down great gullies in the land and pick them up in her mouth and bring them to me. I slung them across my saddle and took them back to the *estancia*, so at least some of them had a chance to live on the milk we managed to take from the cows in the huge herds of nearly wild cattle on the *estancia*. The lambs thought Jean was their mother and when she went out into the garden she was followed by a number of these pets. She also liked the baby beaver which I had as a pet, and kept near the water tank and windmill which provided water for the cattle. The beaver used to run up a plank and swim in the big windmill tank and Jean would follow it and have a swim. But we had to arrange a plank inside the tank so she could get out more easily.

Jean got much too much food from the native servants, they adored her, and she learnt that it was rude to pass wind. The people in the room would say to me 'that dirty dog of yours' and Jean understood that when she made a 'pop' she was not liked, so used to get up quickly and go out into the garden.

One day when I was out riding I saw a ghastly sight, killer dogs had been at the sheep and dozens of lambs and sheep were dead or dying. This is one of the worst things which can happen on an *estancia*, all I could do was to leave Jean guarding the flock and ride back for help to the *estancia*. She was excellent at staying wherever I put her, and all I prayed was that the heat of the day would not be too much for her. It took me seven hours to bring back help and Jean was still where I had put her within a few yards, so I knew she had just done her job keeping the sheep together and staying on guard against the return of the dogs. Jean always took everything in her stride, she learnt new things as if she'd done them all her life. I wonder if any other Dane has ever worked sheep like she did.

Unfortunately, I got very ill in the Argentine and had to go back to England. I didn't take Jean with me because I thought I'd be returning to the Argentine when I got well again and I didn't think quarantine kind. But I never did return, so I wrote to the manager of the *estancia* asking him to have Jean put to sleep so I knew her end. This I thought he had done until thirteen years later I met a man from that area in England and he mentioned a huge Great Dane on an *estancia* out there. He couldn't remember which *estancia* or with whom he saw the dog, so I was tortured wondering what had happened to my Jean. Fate is a funny thing, some twenty years or more later I heard the end of the story. My grandson went to a prep. school and another boy there was from my area in Entre Rios, he told my grandson about a Great Dane his father had once owned called Jean and that was the answer. These English people had adopted her and she died a natural death at thirteen and a half, a very great age for a Dane; what a small world it is! Apparently, they were devoted to her.

2

Jyntee

After the war when we moved to Campions, our home
at Croxley Green, I wanted another Dane. Having been
deprived of a dog for so long under war conditions I
felt now we had a big house and garden that once
again I could own a dog. I saw an advertisement for
some Dane puppies near London and went off to see
them. They were the most dreadful skinny sick-looking
puppies I'd ever seen, but their mother and I just fell
in love with each other on sight. She had big beautiful
eyes and was a fawn with a black mask. She put her
nose into my hand and asked, as plainly as if she had
spoken the words, to come with me; it was only then I
noticed that she only had half a tail. Apparently, that
is how the owner came to have her. The breeder found
the dam had bitten off some of Jyntee's tail at birth
and she was useless for show purposes so was sold to
the present owners who bred with her. I asked if I

could have her instead of a puppy, and the owner looked most surprised and replied that they'd had her six years and they were sure she wouldn't go with me. So I asked them if I went to my car and opened the back door and Jyntee came with me of her own free will, could I buy her? The answer was 'yes', confident she would not go with me. I called Jyntee from the car, she raced to it and jumped in and lay down; she was mine. My two children Patrick and Judith were thrilled when I arrived home with her and Jyntee just fitted in at once.

I noticed that the following Saturday, two days after I got her, there was to be a charity fête locally and one of the events was to be a comic dog show. One class was for the dog with the most tricks, and the children begged me to teach Jyntee some tricks so she could go in for that class. Jyntee was quite amazing, she learnt eleven different tricks in two days, including rolling over, jumping through a hoop, picking her name out of the alphabet, counting by barking on my signal, finding my article amongst others of the same sort put down by other people, and of course easily won the competition. She so enjoyed being clapped, I think all dogs love being clapped. It is routine in my training school when a dog has done right.

Jyntee learnt that cows have horns and can butt rather hard if you get the wrong end of them. She used to help in everything we did on the farm, bringing the calves their milk, bringing in the cows, riding with me when I was schooling ponies, and playing endlessly with the children. They would go and hide and she would pretend she couldn't find them, then suddenly pretend she'd seen them and bound up with a bark. She always lay at the bottom of the stairs in the hall, looking so beautiful. I don't think anyone ever noticed her broken tail. I wrote my first book for my children which was called *Jyntee, the tale of a Dog with a Broken Tail*, so many other children shared Jyntee's adventures when it was published.

All my life I seem to have had bad luck with the animals I love so dearly. Jyntee began to go lame on a back leg and bone cancer was diagnosed. I kept her six months after this, but when I saw that the bone was so fragile that the leg would soon break I had the heartbreaking decision to put her to sleep. My only comfort was that her short life with us had been a very happy one. Before she went I bought Juno, a very nervous puppy who later became known world wide, and was one of the most wonderful dogs ever born, in my eyes.

3

Juno

Juno came to me only because the Dane puppy I had bought from a very big breeder, who was giving up Danes, arrived with a temperature of 105°F. I rang the breeder and told her the puppy was not well and I wasn't going to keep her. I'd just lost my Jyntee and couldn't face another ill dog. So she said she hadn't got another puppy suitable for me, all she had was a brindle bitch of three months who was terribly nervous, so I said I didn't mind nerves, I was sure I could cure those, but I didn't want an ill dog. We arranged to meet at Oxford half way between the breeder's home and mine and exchange puppies. I arrived before the breeder did, and was horrified to see her open her car boot, inside which was this nervous puppy. I took one look at her and I knew she must be mine. No one who loved dogs could let her continue her life in this state of terror. So we swopped the very beautiful sick fawn puppy for the brindle who was to become my Juno.

I wonder where these hereditary nerves come from. Other Danes on the breeder's premises were healthy and didn't look nervous. The fawn puppy was not nervous; why should just one be like this?

If one touched Juno from the back and she didn't see you going to do it, she screamed with continuing yells as if she had been run over. She was rickety but otherwise healthy. I immediately started training her to walk on a loose lead in the town, Woolworths being my main training area. A nervous dog must walk on a loose lead amongst legs and people, shopping baskets, sticky-fingered children who try to pat her and all the rest of the obstacles one encounters in a town. She got quite firm jerks on her choke chain if she sat back. If people touched her she screamed at first, which gave the people an awful shock and hopefully taught them to leave other people's dogs alone. Bit by bit she stopped screaming and began to enjoy her walks in town. I taught her to sit and stay whilst I did my shopping, first of all in the shop where I could watch her reactions to crowds and to people bending to pat her which she soon ignored. Her fear quickly vanished and a confident ignoring of other people made her safe to leave sitting whatever the distractions that occurred.

I then started really obedience training her. Having watched an obedience competition at an agricultural show, I felt certain that Juno could do all those things quite easily. But I realized I should probably join a dog-training club to learn all the ins and outs of show obedience, something I had never done. So by the time Juno was six months old she was confident, happy, longing to learn and a glorious dog to look at, with terrific bone structure, her only two faults being her flying ears and rather thick under-neck. As neither these faults nor any others she may have had from the show point of view mattered for the obedience ring, I felt that should be her initial training.

I took her over to a dog-training club and asked if I could join with Juno. They said, 'No, no Dane could be obedience trained', so rather crestfallen I asked if I could watch that evening's work and I was allowed to. When they came to the advanced work for Test C there were only a few dogs in that class, so I asked if Juno could try one or two of the exercises; I was permitted to try. Juno did them reasonably well and I felt confident I could train her in this work.

I found another club called the West Middlesex, which held its meetings on Sunday mornings at the Master Robert pub at Hounslow, and there I was received with great warmth. The trainers there were quite wonderful, and Juno and I advanced our knowledge in no time at all. Then came the chance of a lifetime for me. The West Middlesex was to challenge to a match the club that had refused me, and we all drew lots for who should represent our club in each obedience test. Juno and I drew Test C, the most difficult test in Obedience, and as luck would have it, I was drawn against the trainer of that club who had refused me as a member, and it was just a few weeks since I'd joined the West Middlesex and started training Juno in competitive obedience. I know it's boasting but I hope it gives courage to the wcak to know that Juno beat the other trainer's Alsatian in the match to win Test C. May this be a lesson to all trainers not to say any dog is untrainable until they have seen whether it is the dog or its owner who needs the instruction most. I have proved time and time again that it is the owners who need much more training than the dogs. So many owners are terribly dull, and their dogs hate working for this reason. Boredom is death to happy work. You need to be outgoing to get the best from any dog, but this does not mean noisy and blustering. I think training clubs could leave the dogs out of the first few lessons and teach owners voice control, signals, and how to be enthusiastic, for to succeed in obedience the dogs must be happy.

4

Getting Into Show Business

People have often said to me, 'How did you start getting your Juno known and into films and television?' This is a long story. The first thing I did was of course to obedience train her. She was one of the first Danes to take part in public obedience competitions, and she always attracted a lot of attention, especially as we also had Chica the tiny little Black and Tan terrier, as the breed was then known, with Juno. This tiny mite would sit between Juno's paws and of course that was just what made a picture for the Press. Without the Press, practically nothing can be achieved. I was lucky enough to meet dozens of charming people from the Press in conjunction with my next book, *Talking to Animals*, when I appeared many times on television with Juno, spoke on the radio and was happy to get a lot of press publicity. It was always Juno who posed for the pictures that were original and were well received by the national newspapers, so the photographers were delighted and used to ring me up and ask me to do some sessions at my home for the magazines and papers. I have literally hundreds and hundreds of photos of my dogs doing just everything. I have ten huge volumes of press cuttings so I shall never really be without my dogs. I only have to open these books and be lost in the world of my Danes.

The next thing I did was road safety. I trained Juno to look both ways before crossing the road and not to cross if there was anything coming. I taught her never to fetch a ball if it ran into the road. I taught her to drop into the down on signal at a great distance to prevent her ever running into the road by mistake even if she was in the country, although I do not advocate any dog being off the lead where there is traffic, however well trained it is. I think only conceited people do this in an effort to show what good trainers they are. Then I started approaching the Road Safety officers in districts within reasonable distance of me, and offered to give road safety training demonstrations for dogs, and talks if they would organize the hall. I borrowed a film on dogs and road safety from the Royal Society for the Prevention of Accidents, and at the end of the talk invited anyone with a dog to let me show them how easy it was to teach it to behave. Slowly I graduated to doing Saturday morning children's cinema matinee performances. In the interval I would take my dogs and draw a white line on the stage and ask the children to shout whether there was a car coming or not. If they yelled 'yes' Juno would not go across the line. If they said 'no' she crossed. The same when we threw an object, if the children said traffic was coming Juno never retrieved it. If the road was clear she would go across and fetch it on command, never without command. The children loved the dogs Juno and Chica and the requests for these demonstrations and talks grew and grew. More press write-ups came our way. Then I decided to start a dog-training class at Croxley Green. I put an advertisement in the local paper asking people to contact me if they would like a dog-training club to be set up with me as trainer. Six people answered and the Croxley Canine Training Club came into being. The only hut we could get on a Sunday morning was the Territorial building at Croxley where the guns were stored, but it was dry and we could do heelwork in the rather confined area around the guns. Juno always demonstrated the correct obedience, and I taught these six people. Soon we were overflowing with requests for training and to cut a long story short I was soon running six clubs in different districts. Every night I ran one within a radius of about ten miles and on Sunday I ran one at my home. Sometimes there were as many as sixty dogs in a class. I used to charge a shilling a lesson to pay for the halls I had to hire in other districts. But mothers and fathers got cunning and I discovered children were borrowing neighbours' dogs and being sent up to me on a Sunday afternoon so that Mum and Dad could put their feet up and let me cope with the children! This was not a good thing as the dogs they borrowed neither loved them nor obeyed them at all and I put a stop to it. Over 7,000 dogs passed through my hands running dog clubs, and Juno was always the dog that showed people how to train their dogs if a demonstration was needed. This led to her being asked to appear at fêtes and give a show of her tricks, etc.; I was delighted to do this. Later Junia even surpassed Juno's efforts at fêtes as she learnt to roll the tombola with her paws and bark as I declared the fête open. She would even pick out the winning raffle ticket because I would have shut my eyes and put my hand in the hat and she of course picked the ticket that bore my scent, but everyone thought it was just clever Junia. I went to Chatsworth and gave a dog-training demonstration with Juno for charity; more press publicity.

Perhaps one of the most amusing things I organized for Juno's publicity to help the Guide Dogs for the Blind was to ask permission to collect at the Championship Cat Show at Olympia one year. Some of the cat owners weren't all that pleased at a dog being at the show, but most of them, knowing how gentle Juno was, were delighted at the television and national newspaper publicity. Juno was put into a cage of baby kittens and adored them. She always had a very motherly attitude to other animals, and when the champion cat was chosen for the supreme prize it lay between Juno's great paws for innumerable photographs to be taken by the Press. We raised quite a considerable amount in Juno's boxes for the Guide Dogs for the Blind. Neither Juno nor Junia ever chased cats, I think they understood that here in our home anything like that was just not on, as did our cat understand that to kill a bird was a crime in our eyes. Birds built their nests at our front door and baby birds flopped about all over the place but neither cat nor

Dane would injure them in any way. Words were enough to teach the two dogs what I wanted, but one good smack taught the cat the only time she caught a bird. I never had to smack my dogs, although I am not one of those sentimental people who say a dog should never be smacked. If I thought a dog warranted that sort of punishment I would do it without regret of any sort. It often shortens the time spent in training when the dog is really doing wrong and not listening to words of reprimand. This doesn't happen if the dog is trained from its earliest days.

I once had to take Juno for an episode of 'The Larkins' for television where there were six cats in the same scene. All the cats were in the kitchen, Juno was to rush in and all the cats were supposed to jump up into different places. This seemed impossible; however, in the end I practised each cat separately and it was achieved, but cats are not easy to work like dogs; food is the best way to get them to do things. The cats didn't belong to me either.

I always remember Juno collecting for the blind at the United Charities Bazaar in the Watford Town Hall. She was a dog who would wag her tail at everyone in the hope they would put money in her boxes. She knew as well as I did that this was something she was supposed to do. One man came up to her and spoke to her and she lifted her upper lip in a warning growl, something I had never seen her do in her life. I told the man to leave her alone and went to the police-man at the Town Hall entrance and asked him to keep an eye on this man. A short time after the man was arrested for shop-lifting. How can a dog sum up character like this and warn me of danger ahead?

I remember one experience with Juno which had extraordinary results. I had left my car in Piccadilly before the age of traffic wardens and, on returning to it, some 200 yards away I saw a man with a key trying to open the door. Juno was police-work trained, I let her off the lead and gave her the command to 'get him' which she swiftly did. I arrested the man and handed him over to a police officer but, and this is the queer story, I got a letter from Scotland Yard telling me they would overlook this instance but I must not put my dog on one of Her Majesty's subjects or I would be liable to prosecution, not being a member of the Police Force (although I trained one of the first Alsatians ever to be accepted by the police in the 1920s and later trained the demonstration Alsatian team belonging to the Thames Valley Police). After this I saw a bank raid at the White City and had Juno with me; I could easily have freed her and possibly have caught one of the thieves but this time I just watched the escape. What a silly law if you are to let your property be stolen and own a dog who could stop it.

Juno and Junia were trained never to bite. The chases they have done in films were always done with actors without padding, for I had trained my Danes only to slip their teeth on to the clothing of the arm, not the flesh. In one film Junia had to catch someone and swing him around her into a hedge, which she did to perfection. In the Montreux Festival winning television entry for the Rose of Montreux, 'Frost Over England', Junia had to chase and catch John Cleese.

He was not padded, but the chase certainly looked frightening and I am sure he said a prayer before he started running, not previously having worked with Junia.

This is how I think dogs should be trained to guard the home. Bark and cease barking on command, attack if given the command, and sit instantly the attacked person stands still without threatening anyone. At the slightest move hold him until he stands still again, have no fear of gun fire, and remain a friendly dog to all until told not to be friendly. The ordinary owner would need years of experience to teach a Dane all this, but it is fun trying.

If film and television people know of a well-trained dog and the property master of the big companies is informed, there may one day be a chance for your Dane to appear on 'the box' or the cinema. You will never be told what to do until they want to film you, you will be treated like the 'property' you are, the hours will be long, the nervous tension killing, but the pleasure of watching your dog will compensate for all this. Occasionally you watch and your dog doesn't appear, you have told all your friends to watch, you've spent a fortune on phoning all and sundry to watch or go to the cinema and your dog is not seen. The cruelty of the scissors on the cutting room floor is quite unbelievable, it's happened to all of us, but carry on, one day your dog may be a star like mine were. Even though I have no Dane now, my cheque book still carries the words 'Barbara Woodhouse and Junia' as a reminder of what she and Juno did for our family.

Originally I did the first B.B.C. pet magazine programme, 'The Smokey Club', which was made in Scotland and I used to go up to Scotland each month on the train with Juno to do it. Juno could not be sneaked into the sleeper as some tiny dogs can be, so we used to find an empty carriage and she would spread out on her travelling rug on the whole length of the carriage seat which just fitted her, and I would stretch out on the other side and we would both sleep the long night journey away and be fit and full of pep for the programme next day. After that I did a training series for commercial television using Juno and Chica as demonstrators.

The next big event was with my baby bull calf Conquest. He was not pedigree but came from one of my best cows and I couldn't bear for him to be slaughtered as was the usual end of a non-pedigree bull calf, so I phoned Richard Dimbleby of 'Panorama' fame and asked if I could bring Conquest, and Juno with him for company, on 'Panorama' and ask for a good home for him with some farmer. This I did. The sight of Juno lying cosily amongst the straw with baby bull Conquest curled up with her head on his shoulder was the most wonderful sight. Six thousand people jammed the B.B.C.'s telephones and also *my* home phone, which number had been given at the end of the programme, for about five hours. Besides this I had 300 letters and dozens of telegrams all wanting Conquest. The silly thing was that quite unsuitable people asked for him. One was a child who wanted him as a pet in the potting shed at the bottom of the garden, one a business man with a flat in London. One application came from a nunnery. One telegram offered me three peacocks in exchange for him. No one seemed to realize that Conquest would one day be a huge bull weighing nearly a ton. Luckily there were some sensible requests and Conquest was given a wonderful home by a Sussex farmer and I hope his progeny improved the herd. Juno really got known after this public appearance on television and her life as a star of stage, screen and television had really started.

People always ask how dog food commercials are done and whether the dog always eats the food or likes the food it advertises, and I always quote what happened with a famous actor doing a beer commercial in which I was involved. He was a teetotaller and nothing would make him drink beer, so Coca Cola was drunk instead. My dog was supposed to drink a glass of beer too: even if I had allowed such a thing, I am sure she wouldn't have liked beer. I certainly would not have any dog of mine doing such an unnatural thing, so she had red gravy to drink.

Once again for this commercial I was called in to do it at the last moment by a desperate producer who rang me and asked me to get in my car and rush up to London instantly, as they'd been trying for over two hours to get the shot, and the Afghan chosen to do the commercial wouldn't do a thing. I rushed up and Juno was bundled out of the car, rushed into the pub where the action was to take place, shown what the action was to be, which was to jump with her forefeet on to the counter and be given half a pint of 'beer' and drink it with the actor drinking his pint at the same time. She did it immediately and I noticed the sweat running off everyone's brows, and I wondered why they were all so het up. I wasn't worried at all. After being paid a miserable £6 for Juno's efforts, someone said to me, 'You silly fool, you should have charged them £50. The actor was getting £1,000, and another £1,000 if the performance wasn't completed by twelve o'clock midday.' It was 11.55 when Juno completed the scene.

Dog food commercials are sometimes a hazard when the camera or actors or clients have difficulties, for no dog can go on eating and eating and eating food however much they like it. On the outside of most tins it gives the right amount for a dog of a certain size for a day. If this is exceeded the dog may get a digestive upset, as anyone might who over-eats. The food in front of the dish has to be made easier to film by being occasionally coloured and sometimes having glycerine over it to make it shine. This is ordinary advertising technique, so the dog mostly eats from the back of the dish if this is done. If the food has to be eaten more times than is good for the dog, due to technical hitches, one of course has to use something else which would not upset the dog by having too much. There is a limit to any dog's appetite so it is usual to take more than one dog of the same breed to the studio. With my Danes this was impossible – everyone knew them from their films and television appearances so I always nagged the production manager to get the camera crew right on their toes and make certain their side of the work didn't let my dog down. In most cases although my dog and I were booked for a day's work it was finished in about two hours. Being Danes they could eat quite a lot anyway!

5

Climbing the Ladder to Success

On reading this book people may imagine that the making of my dogs into film stars was something quite easy. Actually it was slavery. England is not the land of Rin Tin Tins or Lassies, people mostly think of dogs merely as companions, playthings for the children or show dogs, as well as for guarding their property. There must be few people who know the joy I have experienced in training my dogs to almost human intelligence and understanding. I am sure there are many people who own the most intelligent dogs whom they adore and who adore them in return, but I wonder if those dogs would show all that intelligence when asked to act with complete strangers, in strange surroundings, maybe with actors who don't even like dogs and who are only doing their work for a fee. These were the problems I had to cope with, even after I got recognition that my dogs would act with anyone.

The first film I did was for the Children's Film Foundation after being introduced to the boss of a small film company in Dean Street, Soho. He was fascinated by Juno's size and somehow managed to interest Mary Field who was the head of the Children's Film Foundation in this country. She came down to my home to talk to me and be introduced to Juno. The result was that the film company wrote a suitable script called 'Juno Helps Out' and planned it to be performed by my two children Judith, aged eight, and Patrick, aged six, neither of whom had ever acted before, with, of course, Juno as the star.

The company, prior to making the film, came and made one scene here as a try out and it was approved, so shooting started. Our home was turned into a film studio. Great cables passed through our windows and we had to put up with draughts everywhere. The children were worked terribly hard and once Patrick was reduced to tears which made me angry, but the results were lovely and eventually the film made its first appearance at a big cinema in London on a Saturday morning with an invited audience. Juno went on stage after the showing to get the applause of the gathering, and she was launched as the Lassie of England. The film was taken everywhere with Mary Field, as an example of what should be made for children, and took an award at the Venice Festival as the best children's film of the year. It ran on the matinees for years and years, and I believe it is still doing so.

Alas, that was not the commencement of work for Juno as I'd hoped. People still didn't cotton on to the value of a dog to bring in the crowds to the cinemas and I got tired of waiting for the phone to ring with big offers.

One day I was working at Pinewood on 'Appointment with Venus' which was the story of a cow, not a dog, and as usual I only went to the studios if my Juno was allowed to accompany me even though she was not being employed in any way. She always lay on the set watching everything. It was a good training for her future in films to get used to the banging of carpenters, the tension when the words 'All quiet, roll it' were shouted out and the atmosphere that she must have picked up when everyone was on edge.

In between scenes I got talking to the chief cameraman who said the film business was in a poor way and after this film he would be without work. My brain suddenly functioned. I asked him if he'd like to make films for me with Juno and my children. He said he would very much, and that is how I went home to write scripts for six 30-minute films to be shot on 16 mm in black and white. I only wrote outline scripts without actual dialogue because we couldn't afford direct sound. I could only afford to put on a commentary afterwards, so the films had to be so self-explanatory that actual words were of no great importance. The first film, 'Trouble for Juno', was based on the children overhearing their authoress mother reading her new play to their father, and the words 'If we don't raise £5 quickly we'll go to prison'. The son, aged seven, rushed out to tell his sister and they decided to follow the boy scouts' idea of 'Bob-a-Job' and try and raise the money to save their parents from jail. The dog of course took a major part in doing the

35

job they were given of taking a baby out for the afternoon. The adventures that poor baby had to endure would I am sure have raised the mother's hair on end, but the film itself was blown up to 35 mm and shown in most Odeon and A.B.C. cinemas in Britain.

It was followed by 'Juno Makes Friends', a story of the two children befriending an ill tramp whom the dog had found and taking him home and putting him to bed in their beautiful home when mother was out, Juno taking the tramp under her wing, drinking the milk the children had given him, and fetching the bottle of whisky from the dining-room cupboard in exchange. A delightful Poodle puppy was another actor in this film. This film also got bookings on the Odeon and A.B.C. cinemas when blown up to 35 mm. But my money ran out and although I had numerous stories written for a kind of Lassie series, they never got made. Denny Densham, the cameraman who befriended me and made the making of these two films possible, got other work, and eventually started his own company.

At this time I was getting a fair amount of publicity over my autobiography and Countryman Films who made the 'World of Life' series approached me to make a film of my work with animals, like the breaking-in of horses by breathing up their noses, the training of dogs and above all acting by Juno in conjunction with a simple story of our home life with cows, horses, dogs and a chicken. This film took about three weeks to make and was called 'Four Legs to Master'. I never really understood the title, but it had a commentary by Robert Beatty and was accepted as a support film and distributed by British Lion. It may sound conceited but I went and saw it at the Warner cinema, Leicester Square, and sat through two performances. I suppose the first time anyone sees herself on the screen it is a rather awe-inspiring experience. Juno was at her best and the number of 'oh's' and 'ah's' one heard as she did clever things gave me enormous pleasure. I was also delighted to be able to prove you don't have to be cruel or long-winded in breaking-in a horse. The breathing up the nose trick really does work, as I demonstrated with an unbroken horse I had never seen before by getting on its back in about ten minutes after catching it, using the breathing trick taught to me by the Guarani Indians of South America. This film is in the National Film Archives as part of the Heritage of Britain.

I took Juno to both Pinewood and M.G.M. to see the property masters there, for property masters are the powers that be who book dogs which are property as far as films are concerned, unless they are starring in something, when they become actors. The property masters were most impressed with Juno when shown a few things she could do, and whenever there was a chance for her to appear in a film they booked her.

Talking about dogs being property, the system was somewhat different in the B.B.C. If the dog appeared but didn't move, it was property, if it had moving action, it was an actor or actress, and the fees were regulated accordingly. Juno was mostly moving in all the films she did and these began to mount and mount. Directors found her easy to work with. I can't ever remember being given a shooting script before the dog was actually asked to act, which always amazed me.

They all concluded Juno would do the things they asked for. Woe betide me if I ever dared to ask where the dog's entrance would be or exactly what she was supposed to do until just before shooting. I would be brushed aside with an annoyed look inferring that I was a nuisance to say the least of it.

One of the few directors who struck me as being in complete sympathy with an acting dog was the late Mario Zampi with whom I made 'Too Many Crooks' starring Terry Thomas and George Cole. Mario Zampi owned a black Great Dane and always put it in every film he made even if only for a second, and when he met Juno, he kissed her and loved her as if she were his own. When she came to act he described to me what was needed much in advance for her actions which were extremely difficult.

He said to me: 'Please ask the production manager or the carpenters for anything you want for her to do the action more easily.' He gave me time to introduce Juno to the actors which was a very rare concession in film-making. Thus the difficult part, where she had a supposed bottle of chloroform thrown at her by burglars and had to collapse on the floor with eyes shut and the burglars climbing over her without showing any sign of being conscious, was achieved. When this part was first read to me by the production manager he remarked: 'We will, of course, get a vet to give her an anaesthetic so she lies looking dead.' My reply was, 'If Juno can't do this on command she is not going to do it at all.' Both Juno and Junia were trained to close their eyes and feign sleep on the command 'shut eyes'.

In one film at Pinewood I had a horrible experience.

Juno was to go searching for her master in a house built for the film on the set at Pinewood. All I was told was that she should go into the house and stay there until I was told to call her out. What they did not dare tell me was that the house was to go up in flames with my dog in it, and when this happened on shooting the scene (no rehearsal had taken place showing a fire) I made to rush into the house to get my dog out and was grabbed by a man and held. Luckily the dog came on my call and was not injured. This made me simply furious and had there been other scenes with Juno I doubt if I'd have permitted her to act in the film.

Once or twice horrible things in films or television have happened to my dog and I tremble to think what happens to animals who do not have loving owners with them to take care of them and refuse to do anything that may frighten or harm the animal. In the States, I believe, they have someone from their Prevention of Cruelty to Animals Society on all sets where animals are used. Some of the stories I have heard on the use of animals in this country make it long overdue to have the same thing here.

In one film I was working on a cow had to lie down to simulate her calving, and I gently got her to lie down with the trick of lifting one leg and turning the head in the same direction which is the way we teach horses to lie down on command. It just puts the animal off balance and it goes down very gently and seldom objects if someone loving is there to soothe it, but in this case the actress and the cow didn't seem to like each other, and every time she went near it to act with it, it got up. So in the end it was chloroformed and went through the excitable stage before the anaesthetic made it unconscious. It made me terribly unhappy, for she was such a gentle creature and not one of mine. I only owned the calf that appeared in the last scene of that film.

Three other horrible incidents occurred in Juno's acting life. One when she was doing a series for television, a detective story, she had to jump through a glass window after a criminal. Of course, it was not glass in rehearsals, just sugar glass which has no ill-effect on any animal jumping through it, but looks like glass in the finished film. I approached the powers that be to be certain that, on shooting, the glass was sugar glass and I was assured that it would be for certain. I was called to do the action with Juno and sent her through the window as in rehearsal, but the glass was real, not sugar glass at all. The props man had put it in by mistake. Luckily Juno's nails had broken the glass well and truly as her paws hit it and she was not injured, but she could have been severely cut or even blinded.

One other incident that made me annoyed although it was not dangerous to Juno was in an Arthur Haynes comedy. The dog was a witness in a court case about bad cakes or something like that, I forget the exact story, and in the witness box the dog was to eat the cakes with relish. On rehearsal the cakes were unwrapped. On transmission, which was live in those days, the cake she was given to eat was wrapped in cellophane! The dog spat it out and spoilt the action. I'd previously asked the property man to be sure the cake was unwrapped, but the human element enters into all these things. The last incident that showed that Juno was a real trooper was in a sketch with Morecambe and Wise and Juno's action was to rush in and attack. As she rushed in she passed a stage hand carrying a 28 lb weight used to keep scenery in position. It hit Juno's jaw as the man had walked too near her entrance, the dog hesitated for only a second and then ran on stage and did her part as usual. Only afterwards did the huge lump on her jaw show what a truly wonderful actress she was in true tradition that 'the show must go on'.

By now Juno was in tremendous demand. She appeared in films and shows with stars like Alec Guinness, Peter Finch and Adrienne Corri in 'Make Me An Offer'; in series like the 'Invisible Man', 'The International Detective', 'The Avengers', 'Robin Hood', 'Lancelot', etc., and with individual stars like David Frost, June Whitfield, Ted Ray, Roger Moore, Patrick McNee, June Laverick, Odile Versois, Lance Percival, etc. None of the actors or actresses she ever performed with appeared jealous or afraid of her stealing the picture, they rather took the view that more people would probably pay to see the film if a dog appeared and certainly the *Radio Times* and *T.V. Times* used to give her a credit, which I am sure made more people watch the programme.

I made a small film called 'Juno the Home Help' and sold it to Associated Television for children's viewing. I love making films for children and often wonder why more programmes aren't made with dogs in them.

Juno was now leading the life of a human film

star, fetched to the studios in a Rolls-Royce, star on her dressing-room door, written up and used by publicity departments in practically everything she appeared in, and then came the great offer of half a million pounds for her to go to the States and star in a series of sixty-nine television episodes of a series to be written for her. This I could not accept, with quarantine regulations, my beloved dog would be utterly miserable if she had to leave me. Money meant nothing where my dogs were concerned. The fun of working her in films or television was all the reward I wanted. It was a great disappointment not to be able to accept, nor to be able to persuade the company to come to England to do the series.

Another great disappointment to come for me was when Peter Rogers' company of the 'Carry On' series gave me a contract to star Junia in a story I had outlined for her which was to have been filmed after the first 'Carry On' film. Alas for me, the 'Carry On' films were such a success that they never stopped being made and Junia's film was shelved. I got compensation for its non-production which in no way made up for the tremendous disappointment, as it is filming I love, not money. Peter Rogers always said he would like to make a dog picture so perhaps it was a great disappointment for him too, although tempered with the great success of the 'Carry On' series. I think the biggest disappointment of all was when Juno went on location to Cornwall, with Clark Gable for the film 'Never Let Me Go' and the abominable weather only made it possible to shoot two scenes before the company had to return to Boreham Wood and do the scenes in a boat on an artificial lake, rather than on the sea which it was scheduled to do. The producer did not feel Juno could act in a small boat on a lake safely and her part landed up on the cutting-room floor. In any case making this film with Juno was not a happy time as every time Clark Gable forgot his part, some of which had to be written up on a blackboard and held over his head whilst he spoke the lines, he told the director Juno made him forget his lines. This really annoyed me as Juno did everything she was told as always, never fluffing anything, which was more than I can say for some of the humans she performed with in her life.

I well remember one year Juno did an Arthur Haynes Christmas sketch which included pretending to be going to lift her leg against a Christmas tree in a multiple store. Twelve months later Arthur Haynes was suddenly taken ill and the same sketch was put on at a moment's notice. I was phoned at home and asked if I thought Juno would remember her part in that play, as there would be no time or chance of any re-hearsal at all. I rushed her up to London and just got there about fifteen minutes before transmission. I wasn't even allowed to take her on the stage, as the audience were already in their seats and the director said it would spoil the show for them if they saw the dog beforehand. So I prayed I would remember the entries and exits so I could help Juno do the actions by telepathy. I knew her concentration was so great that telepathy with her was an everyday occurrence. The dog went on and did everything correctly including the Christmas tree act, which I think shows dogs can be almost more intelligent and have better memories than some humans.

Juno's life with me must have been one of the busiest any dog ever knew. She was not the sort of dog that had regular walks morning and night as most dogs do or should have. She had to fit in with her public life and that meant running down our common on the grass beside my car at about ten miles per hour. If she wanted to stop a few moments I stopped, but normally she had already been out in the fields with me fetching the cows in and seeing to the calves and horses from about five o'clock in the morning. To keep her fit I considered she should have this mile run on the common at a trot to keep her muscles in good condition, and we always did this before going to the studios and on returning in the evening. She was so trained that never, whatever distractions occurred, would she leave the grass. Juno was never interested in distractions. I think if a hare crossed her path she wouldn't even have looked at it. All animals and birds were her friends so she was never tempted to chase anything living.

I remember once I was going to London early and I'd not been able to give Juno her usual run down the common, so just before Stanmore I put her out on the very wide grass verge to run the half mile of grass there. Suddenly a police car pulled up in front of me and the officer was extremely brusque, he told me it was illegal to let a dog run on the side of the road on the verge and to kindly show him my dog licence. I told him what utter nonsense he was talking and asked for his number, absolutely fuming at being held up

44

when I was in a hurry. I roared up to Scotland Yard, racing up the stairs, and was shown straight into the inspector's office and fumed non-stop for about three minutes about being asked for a dog licence. 'Does anyone carry a dog licence I'd like to know,' I raved. Eventually I ran out of breath, and a very calm and delightful man explained to me that that officer was probably a new recruit and thought he was doing a good job. He assured me he would be told how to behave in future and I left calmly but very late for my appointment. What people don't understand is that if the dog's handler is in any way het up or annoyed she is unlikely to get such good work from the dog as if she were calm. Luckily I am calm when working animals. I remember one write-up I got which said it was extraordinary that I was such a very excitable person normally, yet when with animals I was calm and very patient. I am not sure the writer was right about being patient. I think it is because I am impatient that I get animals to work fast, I don't tolerate bad work or slow thinking, and animals pick up this feeling very quickly and enjoy responding in a like manner.

I never left Juno for the first nine years of my life with her, wherever I went she went. No invitation was accepted unless she was invited too. In fact as the years with her went by people got to asking Juno to things rather than me, knowing full well that would bring me along too. When Juno was nine years old my husband and I had our first ever holiday without a dog. We went to Switzerland for ten days leaving my old Nanny and our children in charge of Juno; they had strict orders not to take her off our place, and she was perfectly well and happy on our return. My husband and I never had another holiday without our dogs as long as they lived.

6

Goodbye, Juno

I suppose I should call myself lucky to have had Juno for eleven and a half years. Danes usually have short lives. She was in superb form all her life. She never went as grey on the face as some Danes do, and I doubt if anyone seeing her working would have known she was over eleven years old. Alas, tragedy was to take her from me.

I got a call from television to take my dogs Juno and little Chica her pal, as well as three other dogs to be collected from people who'd trained these dogs in my school, and go to St Martin's Theatre, London, for filming. I was not told what the dogs had to do but this was not unusual. I got my assistant, Anne West, to come with me. The dogs all behaved perfectly in the train and we got out at Finchley Road station to change trains. There was a train standing with open doors at the opposite platform. I got Chica in and was getting Juno in when without any warning from anyone the doors closed on Juno's tummy, and the train went off with her firmly fixed in the door. Another passenger and I struggled to open the doors but nothing would do this. Never believe that tube trains can't go off without the doors being properly shut. Anne was left behind on the platform with the three dogs. When the train stopped at the next station the doors opened and Juno was freed. She was panting a bit, but I felt that she would best forget this incident if she did some work as she didn't seem hurt. I returned to Finchley Road station and picked up Anne and the dogs and continued with our journey. When we got there Anne recognized Jonathan Routh and said 'Candid Camera', and we realized this filming was to be just one of the episodes used in that programme and came home immediately.

That night Juno didn't seem well. Her heart started pounding a lot. Next day I left her at home with my help whilst I went shopping and on my return the help opened the front door and Juno rushed out to greet me. Before I could kiss her she dropped dead at my feet. People tried to comfort me by telling me how nice it was that she didn't suffer long, nor really grow old, that she'd worked almost up to her death, but I'd lost one of my family, not just a dog. The newspapers wrote up her tragic end, and letters poured in from all over the world. The cast of 'The Avengers' sent me a telegram and a complete stranger sent me this poem:

Ah Juno you have left us all a sense of grief,
No more you pace the city streets or gallop on the
heath.
Yet in those halls where you have gone upon those
higher planes
You take your rightful place once more as 'Juno'
Queen of Danes.

Alan Stockwell

Another acquaintance sent this letter:

Stanmore
1.10.61

Dear Mrs Woodhouse,

We have only just heard the very sad news about Juno, and we both send you our deepest sympathy in your great loss.

On each dreaded occasion when our dog has been taken from us we have suffered an indescribable void in our hearts. Bearing in mind Juno's exceptional capabilities and striking personality we can well imagine how greatly you will miss her.

If there is any consolation at all it is that you gave Juno a very happy life which she might not have otherwise had. And by your skill you were able to bring out a talent which was surely unique in the dog world.

Juno will long be remembered by all who had the good fortune to meet her as a most impressive example of how close an association can develop between the mind of dog and owner. Certainly a harmony which we shall never forget as long as we live.

Yours sincerely,
(signed) Mary Leighton

Juno lies buried in my garden, one of the most precious friends I've ever owned.

7

The New Arrival

After Juno died my husband begged me to get another
dog quickly. I didn't feel like doing this at all. I was
devastated, but he was right, and when Mrs Davies of
the Oldmanor Danes offered me a bitch puppy out of
a litter she had with two brindles in it, I went up to see
them. The moment I set eyes on the bold puppy that
came out to greet me I knew she must be mine. Both
her parents were champions and she had the deep
golden undercoat and tiger markings that I so love. She
was just six weeks old. She came in the car with me
lying contentedly on a rug on the seat and slept most
of the way home.

Junia I called her. I couldn't use the name Juno
again, it was sacred to that lovely dog now gone. I had
to choose a name that meant something and this surely
did. I always shortened it to Juni because the 'i' at the
end made it easy for the puppy to identify herself

with that name. Junia would have had one syllable too many for quick communication. And Junia, if I had anything to do with it and had any luck at all, would follow in Juno's footsteps as nearly as I could train her to do so. But the extraordinary thing was she somehow seemed to know what to do. I only had to show her once and she instantly did the thing that would normally take a puppy some weeks to learn. I had a feeling my Juno had come back to me inside this amazing puppy.

Chica, our little Black and Tan terrier, took to her at once and played endlessly with her although she herself was nearly twelve years old, and I have the joy of having all these early days of Junia and Chica in a film called 'A Star is Made'. This had cinema showing, and lots of 16-mm copies have gone out all over the world. No one can deny that lovely intelligent look on Junia's face, and the way she does the tricks that Juno did and which she performed for this film so naturally that anyone seeing it would imagine all the actions were as Junia thought them up. Junia was different in character from Juno. Juno was always a placid dog; Junia was always wanting to do things, her ability to learn and do was unending.

When Junia was four months old M.G.M. rang me and said they wanted a Dane for their new film 'Kill or Cure' to star Terry Thomas and Eric Sykes with quite a demanding part, including an attack from the Dane; had I got one? I looked at Junia and asked them if I could bring her to see them, as although she was only four months old they didn't want a dog for another five weeks, and knowing how Danes grow, I felt Junia might by then be big enough. I knew I could train her to do anything I wanted, or rather they wanted, because she already knew so many things including an attack on a supposed criminal, was completely unafraid of gunfire, and knew up to distant control in obedience which she loved. Her brain was so big the sky was the limit.

George Brown, the production manager, and the director looked at her and at once said, 'Yes, providing she grows enough,' so that was that. Junia ate everything, her rate of growth was tremendous, so at the appointed date we took her to M.G.M. at Boreham Wood to be seen, and the contract was ours. The coincidence was, Juno's first feature film assignment was with Clark Gable for M.G.M. and now Junia's first feature film was to be for M.G.M. too. I felt she was to follow exactly in Juno's footsteps.

The film was a great success. Terry Thomas and Eric Sykes are utterly delightful to work with, and I thoroughly enjoyed doing the film. Junia never fluffed anything she was asked to do, and did it on command or signal without noticeably looking at me. She was made a tremendous fuss of by everyone at the studios and I was even given the cameraman for a few seconds to take a short piece of film of her first meeting with the stars, to put in my film 'A Star is Made'. She was a little over-awed at first, but soon realized what she had to do and from then onwards Junia's film career commenced and she took over from Juno.

Junia's first starring part in a film called 'Beware of the Dog' was with a boy of about nine years old and the pair worked extremely well together, but then the boy loved dogs and listened to all I told him.

What many people don't recognize in films is that nothing is done naturally, everything is done in response to some command or order from the handler. The best dogs take these signals or commands with hardly a glance in the handler's direction. It is rather fun to watch a dog working in a film and see if you can spot where the handler is standing from the upward flick of the eyes of the dog. I always tried to train both Juno and Junia from behind, if I was allowed to speak to them, so they didn't look at me. Very often the sound is on, and the lighting such that it makes it impossible to talk, and sometimes to signal, so you have to work out communication by telepathy by just thinking what the dog has to do, and if she is in tune with the handler she will do what you are thinking about.

Very often when doing commercials the actors are children, and my Danes always liked working with them. The children never seemed even slightly afraid of my dogs, nor were the parents, who could have been more difficult to deal with than the children.

The worst part about dogs acting with children is that the children tire very easily, and are often bribed by the mothers, who are usually with them, to do things until the poor children are nearly sick with eating too many sweets. I never bribe a dog that is working because its saliva would run, and its tummy would expect a meal which it couldn't have and it eventually would end up with indigestion. Danes must work for love and praise which they lap up.

Give a working dog, whether it be in films, the show ring, or obedience, as much rest as possible between work, preferably in the car or dressing-room, so that it comes fresh to whatever needs to be done when it is called.

Dogs have to be made up very often the same as actors and actresses. Junia developed grey hairs on her muzzle at two years old and had to have Max Factor's black pancake to hide them. The make-up man made her up just the same as the human star, for all make-up is a highly skilled profession, and on film sets only the make-up man can do it by the rules of his union. I remember once Equity writing to me asking me to join that union for the dogs, but I did not think this was necessary. People were always delighted to employ my Danes and never argued about what I asked in fees. Actually I was so happy working dogs in show business that I am sure I never asked enough.

One of the troubles with film-making is the locations chosen. They could be right amongst sheep or chickens, so the dog must be trained to ignore everything but the handler's commands and the actor she is working with. One film I remember was in a field with a huge wild carthorse who insisted on galloping at Junia at full speed, and then turning its heels on her and kicking out as hard as he could. I implored the director to have it caught and tied up and he was quite nasty to me, and told me my dog should ignore that sort of thing if it was properly trained. I tried to explain it was that I was worried in case my beloved dog got hurt, or the child she was working with got hurt, but this fell on deaf ears. In the end I 'went on strike' and caught the horse myself and tied it up. The director only spoke to me after that if he really had to. Some directors are very tedious to work with.

To further Junia's career I informed all the property masters of film studios and television companies that she was available for work and the first television she did was an interview on Hobbies Club for the B.B.C. when she did a few tricks. Then I met a director who was interested in starring her in a film he wished to write, and the director was to be one who had made some of the Lassie television series in America and who had read about Junia and wanted to use her in films.

The contract was signed for a serial to be shot near Brighton, and it would take five weeks to shoot. Junia had to have a 'stand-in' in case anything happened to her in the middle. I chose Tina, a Dane bitch that belonged to a friend of mine, Ron Pegley, of Radlett. She had never acted before but that didn't worry me. I knew I could soon teach her if she was used. In any case dog stars have stand-ins for doing the donkey work like standing in position when the lighting is being done on the set; the star mustn't get tired.

We settled with the film company that they would arrange accommodation for Junia, my young son Patrick who would help me, and Ron Pegley and his Dane Tina. Patrick and I went down to Brighton two days before filming was due to start, but when I asked the production manager where we were supposed to stay, he said he'd made no arrangements. He'd thought we were making our own. This was utterly ridiculous as it had been agreed that we'd be in a hotel. The trouble was it was August and no hotel had a room to spare, especially for a party like mine with three people, a miniature Black and Tan puppy and two Great Danes. I was desperate.

I was driving up a narrow street and saw a notice on an empty terrace house 'For Sale' with a house-agent's address on it. I went into a phone box and told a rather astounded man at the end of the line that I was desperate for somewhere to live for five weeks with our dogs, etc. Could he let me have this empty house if I hired furniture for it? He said they were not the people to ask but if I liked to give him the number of the phone box where I was, he would phone the owner and ask him, and he'd get the owner to ring the phone box. I waited about ten minutes and, sure enough, the phone rang and a man's voice told me he'd heard about my plight and if I liked to stay where I was, after explaining to him where I was, he'd come around in his car and see me. A very few minutes later, a man turned up. He said he could not let me have that house as it had no facilities at all and no furniture. However, if I would follow him to the sea front where he owned a whole block of flats, in which recently one tenant had died and one flat was therefore unoccupied, I could have it if I wished. We could hardly open the door of the flat, it was so full of junk. It was a huge place with two bedrooms, sitting-room, two bathrooms and kitchen space, and smelt of junk and old age, but it was a roof over our heads.

This man was one of the kindest people you could possibly meet anywhere. He loved dogs and immediately said if we came down the following day, he'd send his Spanish servants there to tidy up and he'd get rid of most of the furniture and send some decent stuff up for us. I asked what rent he wanted and he said, 'What can you afford? £10 a week?' I could hardly believe my ears. Next day we came to the flat and never have I seen such a transformation. It was clean and completely adequate for our needs. We set about stocking food, for instead of the luxury of a hotel it was obvious that not only would I have to do filming but cooking for us all. The owner said he'd send his Spanish maids in to do the daily cleaning; more kindness. I couldn't believe that such generosity existed from a complete stranger.

I got in touch with the film company and the production manager came round to see us. I had not had a shooting script, only an outline story and when I asked for a script one couldn't be produced that day, but this was something that I was already used to.

We were to be on location at a farm, at 8.30 the following morning. We got up very early and I made the breakfast, then we all took the dogs about a mile away to a huge recreation field at Black Rock, for their exercise, which we had found the night before. Little Mini, our tiny four-months-old Black and Tan terrier, successor to Chica, was also in the film and to see this tiny mite rushing after the huge Junia was quite funny. She was very intelligent and I felt would do what was asked of her. The owner of the house on location didn't seem at all pleased with all the people striding through his house, etc., and said his wife was terribly ill and would we keep quiet. Junia had to bark many times at the door of the house and he came out and asked us to keep quiet and stop the dog barking. I felt terrible as I realized how much noise Junia made when she barked, and worried about the number of times she was asked to repeat the performance for technical reasons. The owner seemed to think I had control of what I had to do in spite of me telling him I was only the dog handler.

In one part of the film a lot of dogs had been hired elsewhere and their action was supposed to be to rush into the house and out again at a given signal. Alas, not having had their breakfast they made a bee-line for the tent which housed the food for the actors and crew of the film and in a few minutes the food was eaten, which caused some headache for someone.

Junia did one quite inexplicable thing. The director was reading to me for the first time the script where it described Junia's next action, and as he read it to me, without being shown anything or given any command, Junia went and did the action. I involuntarily told the cameraman to 'roll it', having directed films myself and seeing that the dog was going to do a perfect take. The action was to go to the row of kennels, take off the padlock, drop it and undo the kennel door by pulling off the hasp with her teeth and let little Mini out. The director was very angry with me. He said, 'Since when did the dog handler give my cameraman the order to shoot film?' I was very apologetic, but in the finished film they *did* use that shot, so perhaps I ought to have been thanked, not scolded.

Junia was at her best. She did everything she was asked to do, many of the things being extremely difficult for a seven-months-old puppy, but the whole atmosphere of the filming was unhappy. The wife of the owner of the house died in the middle of filming. Poor little Mini nearly died too, for when she and Junia had to come rushing out of a stable together, Junia's back leg hit her full on the head, and she collapsed, I thought she was dead. I picked her up and quickly realized her neck had been put out of joint. Luckily my knowledge of bones and discs saved her. I put her neck in and she came round and, after being shaky for a short time, completely recovered and did her part magnificently in the film, and much enjoyed doing it. She was so tiny everyone loved her.

The film progressed with constant trouble. There were quite a lot of children in the film and some got ill, the chaperones were upset and wanted to go back to their stage school, and we found the atmosphere difficult to work in.

Patrick one night woke up with a terrible sore throat and high temperature. I managed at midnight to contact the mobile doctor service that existed in that town, and a very charming doctor came to see him immediately, and gave him an antibiotic. But the trouble was that next day I had to leave him alone in the flat to go filming, and when I asked to be allowed to go home in the lunch hour and see him and give him something to eat, I was forbidden to go, which upset me terribly. However, Ron Pegley offered to go and returned after giving Patrick his lunch, with the report that Patrick seemed better and was reading a book, so I felt happier.

That night I lay awake semi-listening to Patrick, in case he needed anything, and I heard men at about two o'clock go into the flat below and start talking.

Well, I knew the flat below was empty; it belonged to someone abroad, I'd been told. I listened to snatches of talk and I had a strong feeling the people talking were connected with the Great Train Robbery. I went down to the flat and knocked on the door, and three men opened it. I asked them to keep quiet as I was trying to get to sleep in the flat above. They left the flat at 3 a.m. Next night the two o'clock visit and departure were repeated, and I told the police my suspicions. A detective came to see me but pooh-poohed the whole idea. The men never came again, but the next morning some of the missing mail-bags were washed up on Black Rock beach. I have always wondered if I was right.

The child star of the film was a boy who'd never acted in his life before, but he was a nice intelligent child, and got on with Junia very well. Charles Tingwell was his supposed father and Michael Balfour a crook in the film. He is an actor I've always been very fond of. He is wonderful to work with and loves dogs. What a difference it makes to have someone who loves dogs in films.

I felt very unhappy working in that film. The director never said a word of praise to anyone throughout the whole of the filming. I asked him one day why he didn't ever praise the dog or the children and his reply was: 'If I say print it that means I am satisfied and that's all that is needed in film-making.' I am afraid I didn't agree. A little enthusiasm and praise goes a long way with dogs and children, let alone grown-ups. The film was finished and we thanked our kind landlord for his wonderful help and great kindness and left Brighton for home. We saw the film some months later and I personally found it tedious, the constant medium shots and the slowness of the film could, I felt, have been much improved on the cutting-room floor. But Junia's part pleased me. The critics said 'Dog beautiful, children natural, background pleasant', so I suppose someone liked it. Another said 'Junia the Great Dane a truly beautiful and intelligent heroine', so I was satisfied.

8

The Rise to Stardom

Junia's fame was spreading, by now she had two huge volumes of press cuttings. She appeared in many television shows, 'Animal Magic', 'Wednesday Magazine', the Lance Percival show, etc., and then joined 'The Avengers' for two episodes – 'Death of a Great Dane' and 'Concerto', again following in Juno's footsteps. She did a play with Ted Ray called 'Happy Family' and the *Radio Times* repeated Brian Sears' remark: 'She is such a superior actress that we used her in spite of her being a bitch, not a dog. At one point she had to bark in reply to Ted and she was right on cue, so in the script we call her Junior which is masculine but doesn't confuse the animal.' Actually I was controlling Junia by telepathy throughout the transmission which was live, so I couldn't speak anyway to her. It wouldn't have confused Junia whatever they'd called her.

I once gave a dog-training class and never used the usual words of command like sit or stay. I used the names of vegetables just to prove that it is what the owners are thinking rather than what they say which makes the dogs respond. Without telepathy in my life with my Danes I'd not have been able to achieve one half of what they did in show business. Once Juno had to bark in time to a song called 'Dog's Day' sung by Tommy Cooper in a programme called, if I remember rightly, 'The Stars Came Down'. Juno never failed to be right on time with her bark.

Junia, of course, barked on my blinking my eyelids, if it were possible for her to see me blinking, which it often wasn't! This was even more certain of success than telepathy. I was, of course, always slightly nervous that some unrehearsed happening would distract her attention for a second. This once did happen when Honor Blackman was doing an episode with her and she missed the cue to jump on a sofa, owing to a stagehand having dropped an aluminium ladder in the background. This was just enough for a young dog to lose her concentration for a second or two, and the director seemed quite angry with me instead of being angry with the stage-hand. But with animals in show business there is far less patience shown to dogs than to human actors and actresses. The dog is given many less rehearsals, sometimes no rehearsals at all.

Show after show cast Junia. 'Beggar My Neighbour' with June Whitfield was a happy one as were nearly all the assignments with her. I have lots of thank-yous from producers which made my life happy, for by nature I am a perfectionist and I worry terribly if anything I do is not up to my own set standard. Junia now got requests to do dog food commercials, and be photographed with beautiful models. The one I enjoyed most was the *Sunday Times* mannequin show. Junia stood for publicity photographs on an island in the middle of Park Lane, attracting much attention from passing motorists, causing one or two nearly to hit each other.

I was often called to pick up the pieces on a production. I think expense is what causes some companies to choose amateur dogs instead of professional ones, forgetting sometimes that the cost of wasted film stock and time probably costs much more than employing a well-trained dog and experienced handler.

I was called one day to do something quite simple for Junia, which was to jump through a screen of white paper which was supposed to be a wall. For two days, I'd been told, they'd struggled with another dog who wouldn't do it. This was an easy thing to get a dog to do, with one rehearsal to show her it was only paper.

Ken Russell directed a film, 'The Diary of Nobody', with Junia taking the dog's part, and he seemed worried how Junia could be made to lick the boots of the star. I simply rubbed a piece of cooked meat on the boot to be licked and gave her the command 'licky, licky' which she did happily. You may wonder why I say 'licky, licky', not 'lick'. I always use an 'i' or a 'y' at the end of a command if I possibly can; the dog's ears pick up that sound much more easily than the 'k' at the end of 'lick'.

Junia did commercials for masses of different products, from the Gas Council to the selling of cars, horse feed and cookers. She appeared at multiple stores, lectures, fêtes, schools, etc., besides all her work in films and television. Sometimes the fees she got were in keeping with her star status, at other times she worked for a pittance for a small film company with a tiny budget. Money never really bothered me, it was the fun of achieving something and being so proud of Junia that I worked for.

Always my mind was on one big thing and one big thing only. I wanted to star Junia in a big colour film. It looked as if this ambition would never be achieved, so in a case like this there is only one thing to do, do it oneself. I sat down and wrote a script about a miner's son who wanted to become a pop star, and who, on hitch-hiking to London, stopped for the night at a farm where he met a Great Dane who had been taken in by the farmer's wife, when found wandering on the farm, obviously abandoned by a motorist going on holiday. The adventures of this lad and the dog and the boy's hopes and disappointments in his efforts to become a pop star were the plot of the story. I tried to get professional script writers to help me put my outline in order, but I was too small fry. Either they simply replied they didn't do other people's script ideas, or they weren't interested. Luckily in the end someone told me about Don Nicoll who lived in Rickmansworth, and he enthusiastically took up my idea and wrote the shooting script. The next thing to do was to find a boy capable of doing the part with a really lovely voice, for it was to be a semi-musical. I wrote to Mickey Most about it and he put me in touch with the publicity expert for a famous pop group. Here is where a new era started for me and Junia.

9

Film-making

David, the publicity expert, was most helpful. He said he'd heard a boy sing at a hotel in Sanderstead with a small group, who, he thought, had great talent. Would I like to meet him? Of course I agreed and the boy was brought to see me. He was a handsome fifteen-year-old with a fantastic voice; the power of it for one so young was amazing. But the boy was rather quiet and could not readily smile, as I would have liked him to do or so it seemed to me. But I thought it was worth a go, and I became his first manager. David and I started a company and he would do the publicity. I had the boy stay in my home and taught him all I knew (I'd done repertory in my youth for a short time). I got him on loving terms with Junia and soon David's efforts were rewarded with masses of press write-ups. The fact that this boy was to star in a film with my dog brought most of the pop magazine pages clamouring for publicity pictures, and I spent hours thinking up new locations and new actions that would produce the greatest amount of exposure for the boy. His own name was unsuitable so we gave him the name Jonny Ross, and that was how all his publicity went out.

The production of the film was in my hands and solely at my personal expense. No one would back my hunch that this boy and dog were stars of the future. The cost of the filming, taking studios with a full crew, the booking of actors like Larry Burns, Alan Gifford, Vic Wise, George Woodbridge, Fred Griffiths and actresses as gifted as Jo Robottom and Hilda Fenmore plus many more, made the budget quite a big one, although I shall always be grateful for the exceptional kindness over their fees shown to me by the cast, which made it possible for me to eventually succeed in this highly competitive business. The music was a big problem. Here Norman Newell helped me by coming to my rescue, allowing me to use 'Along the Way' already written specially for Jonny Ross for the flip side of a record he made. The title of the film 'Along the Way' I used from the record. Peter Ramsay, a young friend of mine, wrote some of the music. The rest I got from music libraries. Geoff Love proved the kindest possible person. He came to the recording studio and helped me to get Jonny to sing correctly my hymn 'By Your Side'. In the beginning 'Along the Way' has the boy singing in a little Welsh chapel the solo hymn, and when I thought I had found a suitable hymn to use the publisher wanted £500 for the use of a few lines, so the only thing to do was to write a lyric myself and I asked Hero de Rance to write the music for it. We collaborated only over the telephone. I would read her the lyric and she would hang up the phone and go and write some music and play it back to me over the phone. She was very clever at doing this and in no time at all we had the right tune for the lyric which was used in the film. Not only that, the hymn got published by Ascherwood, Hopwood and Crew and was twice sung on the radio, and also by the Wimbledon Girls' Choir in Belgium. It is a very simple hymn.

By Your Side

God is with you every day and through the long dark
    night,
If you're sad or lose your way, he's there to put things
    right.
It's often hard to understand that life can hurt you so,
But God is there to take your hand, and help you as
    you go.

The voice of God is always clear, the path of right is
    wide.
When you need Him, He is near, so let Him be your
    guide.
His love enfolds you every day, your hope is in His
    hand,
He will help you on your way, as by your side He'll
    stand.

The filming started on location in the Lake District. The weather forecast was appalling, but I've always had weather sense and this has been proved time and time again in the weather we got on my training courses. In the last fourteen years I've only had three days with any rain at all on a course and that is right through the year. This weather instinct is a sort of gift, I think. I rang the Meteorological Office for a forecast for the Lake District and they said heavy rain. But I still thought they were wrong and backed my hunch and the crew set off in their vehicle, and Junia and I and my son Patrick, who acted as my aide-de-camp, set off to follow them in my estate car. It was pelting with rain when we set off, but slowly got better and better as we got farther north. By the evening it was fine but overcast. Next morning it was brilliant sun and we filmed all day everything that was necessary in the most beautiful light you could possibly have. We filmed amongst daffodils, mountains and lakes and the result would have made a travelogue if it had never reached the cinemas as a second feature. Junia enjoyed her actions and by the evening we were exhausted. The poor cameraman was nagged to hurry up all the time as I knew instinctively that we only had that one day to film all we needed, as I felt it would rain the next day. Unlike productions which have backing, I could never afford to wait for weather, any extra expense would have put my film out of reach from a financial point of view. Every shot had to be 'take one or two'. No wasting of time, stock or action was possible if the film were to remain within the budget I'd accepted. My predictions came true; it was pelting with rain the next day, but we'd finished all we needed in one day and returned to do studio work. I'd taken studios at Bushey for a week and the film had to be completed studio-wise in that time. I won't go into the worries and troubles of making a film. I think I suffered them all. Had I known of the snags nothing on earth would have made me venture on such a production. However, most things were overcome until tragedy befell me after the shooting was finished and the film had gone to the cutting-rooms.

I was stationary in my car in a village twelve miles from my home when suddenly I was hit in the back of my car by a big Humber car which apparently couldn't stop when it saw something coming in the opposite direction. Junia was in the back of my car and I had a passenger in the front. Somebody called an ambulance and my passenger was taken to hospital, but I was not taken because I refused to go without Junia. The ambulance men said they were not allowed to take a dog in an ambulance so I was left in the car with Junia with tremendous shock and a hurt spine, but not dangerously injured in any way. Nobody suggested rescuing me until a bulldozer came along and the driver got down and came over to the car and asked me what had happened, seeing the smashed car. The driver of the other one had gone to call the police. I was crying with shock and this workman from the bulldozer was kindness itself. He held my hands and comforted me and eventually a car stopped with three firemen in it, who asked if they could do anything. I told them what had happened and said no one would take me to the hospital because I had my dog. They offered to take me to the nearest hospital which they'd be passing, which was a mental one, but at least it had a doctor there. They took Junia too and dropped me at the entrance. I walked very shakily into the hospital and the porter asked the house-surgeon to come and see me. A very casual young doctor came up to me and said, 'My goodness, you look ill. What's happened?' I told him. He never examined me or helped in any way whatsoever, but left with the remark: 'You'd better get home and see your own doctor.' There was no suggestion that I should be helped with getting home some twelve miles away with a Great Dane dog.

One of the patients in the mental hospital luckily passed me and Junia, and stopped to pat her, saying: 'Is that the dog I see on the telly?' and when I said 'Yes', he said, 'You look ill. What's the matter?' So I told him and he immediately went off and phoned for a taxi for me and stayed with me until it came, for which I shall always be grateful. The taxi took me home and I shut Junia in the sitting-room and dialled 999 and an ambulance took me to hospital. Once again nobody seemed to care. I suppose had I been bleeding copiously or had only one leg they might have done something for me, but I was just left lying shivering cold until a nurse arrived with another young doctor. To my amazement the nurse started chatting to the doctor about whether he liked her new hair-do. I told him my back and neck hurt a lot, but a cursory examination brought only the diagnosis that if I rested I'd soon be all right, and I was told to go home. As it turned out, I'd got a severe whiplash injury to my neck and displaced a disc in my back. It took me a very long time to get even partially over this incident for my brain kept shutting out. I tried to continue cutting the film with the editor, but was often reduced to tears with the strain of not being able to remember, so in the end we stopped the cutting after the rough cut.

The next few months were a nightmare. I was terribly worried about the financial side of the film, and then the blow fell. Jonny Ross's progress to fame had been going ahead thanks to David's and my efforts until in every write-up he was called the Cliff Richard of the future. All looked very promising for Jonny. Then he and his father decided his career could do without me. Here was I faced with the fact that I had put £17,000 into starring this boy in a film in the belief that he would be a success, and the film would be wanted, and now, before it had even been shown to a distributor, he was leaving my management of him. I never heard of anything happening to him for some time. When he did succeed and became one of the New Seekers I was delighted for him. I always felt that he had a lovely voice, but my idea for his place in the pop world had been that he and Junia should always appear together as a gimmick. Junia was already a star in her own right, and what could appeal to the public more than a dog and a boy together? But of course it never came off.

Eventually, after about a year and a summons against the driver of the car that hit me, I was awarded £2,000 damages out of court for the accident, but this would never compensate me for the injury to my back, although people seeing me training dogs would hardly guess that I had been so hurt.

I have always had a tremendous amount of will-power and my mother brought us up on the Coué system, 'Every day and in every way I am getting better and better', and it works, for with the exception of having two children, in the last thirty-seven years I have never had one day in bed, because my animals could never spare me. I always remember having an operation on my foot and arranging for it to be done at eight o'clock at night when my animals were all safely settled for the night, and I was determined to go home by 8 a.m. to milk my cows and take my dog out. The matron of the hospital almost wrung her hands that morning and said never had anyone been allowed out so soon and started to help me down the stairs. Unfortunately she tripped and fell and I had to pick her up.

If I have 'flu I have a theory that doctors would not agree with. I believe if you stay in bed the virus just loves the warmth, etc.: the perfect conditions for multiplying. I don't give them this pleasure; I keep up and about and go out in the cold. They hastily leave for the next victim. So far I've never suffered any setbacks by carrying out my beliefs. In fact if my back gets too bad I say a prayer that a big dog will turn up who really pulls on the lead. I give it one terrific jerk on the choke chain, the dog comes back to heel and my disc returns to its proper place. I suppose this action is exactly the opposite to what happened to me in the car accident and is therefore the answer to my problem.

The film cutting and editing of 'Along the Way' was eventually finished, the sound put to it after terrific differences of opinion with the studio who did the recording. I have discovered that in the film business people have set ideas which are difficult to overcome. Once I got so cross with a sound studio over another film I made that the man who was doing the recording of the volume said he wouldn't work with me – I could do it myself. What he didn't know was that I could jolly well do it myself, although I'd never done it before, and I got what I wanted. Thank goodness that studio was not one that belonged to any union or the whole lot would have been out on strike. I don't like being challenged without taking up the challenge, that is why I think dogs know they'd better not challenge me. I can never understand why people who are being paid to do a job have to try to put their ideas over on the person who is doing the paying, but that is life these days.

I shall never make another film, with all the snags in the trade, like going slow and wasting time so that double overtime rates can be paid. These have been hazards in some of the films I have made in my life. When you've only a limited amount of money to spend, probably all borrowed, and you see your house in danger of being taken from you by the bank, it is all too worrying. I love making films, I'd love to make a series on my training of dogs, so that when I do the 'down stay' myself and go to join my beloved dogs, at least my method of training, which is different from anyone else's, might help future generations of dogs and owners, but unless I win the Premium Bonds' biggest prize this is never likely to come about.

One queer part of my car accident was that the bulldozer man kept ringing me up to find out how I was, and eventually wrote me amorous letters, which I didn't answer, he knew I was happily married and not quite his cup of tea! Then one day I had a letter from him asking for a copy of my autobiography *Talking to Animals* and the heading was Armley Gaol! He told me he was there on a charge of manslaughter, having been in a pub brawl in which a man was killed. I never heard the result of the case as I felt that I had to stop answering his letters, but I felt certain he'd get off. I did send him a copy of *Talking to Animals*, and I wondered how on earth a man with the kindness and gentleness that this rough diamond showed me could have got into this mess.

Now that my mind had recovered, I was able to try to sell my film to a distributor. Everyone said I'd never succeed for the modern trend was violence, sex or war, and my film was a family one with a 'U' certificate. People were right. Distributor after distributor turned my film down; some said it was enjoyable but too naïve. One big circuit merely said: 'Unfortunately the distribution people have come to the conclusion that they cannot see their way clear to handle the film, so it is with much regret I have to tell you that we cannot be interested in the distribution or exhibition.' The writer kindly added: 'It was nice meeting you and I am very sorry that I cannot help you on this occasion, but let us hope there will be another opportunity in the future.' This and all the other refusals put me into despair. The bank wanted the borrowed money paid back. I had no hope of recouping one farthing for all I had spent on Jonny Ross. The £2,000 damages from my accident helped, but there was still a long way to go. I just had to work harder. Dogs came in and out of here almost on a conveyor belt. I'd train up until ten o'clock at night. Then my luck changed and my books were sold for publication to America and the advance royalties paid off my debts. A chance remark of a film projectionist that M.G.M. E.M.I. Distributors were looking for family films made me take it along to them to view and they accepted it as a second feature. I had a charming letter from the manager of a cinema near Oxford which said: 'I viewed the film and thought it very pleasant. I shall try and book it again for a children's matinée in the near future.' Another letter from the manager of a Regal Cinema said: 'It was indeed a pleasure to present a film free from the usual sex and violence. Junia was certainly popular with my patrons. I hope your production will continue to give pleasure to many people.' There was one manager somewhere who wrote to the distributors and said his cinema suffered badly from the showing of my film and his other cinemas would cancel their bookings. I felt this was a very unfair thing to say. Surely the feature film is the cause of people going to the cinema or not. I doubt if anyone even knows what the second feature is before they see it. However, there are always entirely opposite points of view. The manager of a cinema in Herefordshire wrote to me: 'When I book another programme later in the year which should take money, I will ask for your film as a support for it.' I felt how terribly nice it was of these and other managers who wrote to me to take the trouble to cheer up a new and insignificant independent producer. My great day was when the film came on for a week at the Classic Cinema at Hampstead and the manager went to town with a promotion for it. Although to all the producers who get a circuit release my rewards must seem small, at least I proved to myself that there are still people in this country who would rather see a lovely dog acting than a film swamped in sex.

10

Action Stations

I hope people reading this book won't think I exploited my dogs in show business. The training of them was the greatest joy to me and to them. Nobody who ever met my dogs or worked with them could doubt that to work with a loved mistress and to receive the praise and adoration they received from all and sundry must be a happy life for any dog.

The teaching of the actions that the dogs would need in their work was purely a matter of finding what made them do things. For example, I found it difficult to teach Junia to howl. She would whine but didn't catch on that that was not enough. Howling shows unhappiness and Junia was never unhappy. Then luck came my way and a Jack donkey was put in my neighbour's field. He brayed incessantly and Junia hated this noise and set up a big howl of irritation. This was my chance. Every time she howled I said 'Howly' and she soon knew what to do. My tone of voice when giving her that command was almost a howl too. Tone of voice matters terribly; the excited tone for a chase, a tired tone for a yawn, a curious tone when she had to dig up the ground, and a sleepy tone for when she had to shut her eyes and feign sleep on command.

It is terribly tiring teaching a dog new things, not only for her but for me. Great concentration is necessary and instant change of mood when the dog is succeeding in doing what I want. Dogs who are not really as one with their owners or handlers are unlikely to learn quickly. A tremendous bond has to exist between them. If one is upset it is useless trying to teach a dog anything; if one is frightened for any reason that fear will communicate itself to the dog by scent. Worrying over something also communicates itself to a dog. So in fact dog training, especially in show business, is not all honey. One of the most difficult things to cope with is the admiration the dog gets on the studio floor. Everyone wants to talk to her or pat her and this tires the dog. Yet the atmosphere on the set is good for the dog. If she is put into a dressing-room she just relaxes and goes to sleep and it takes a good run in the open air to wake her up. Sometimes the director will change the action the dog has to do in the middle. It may be she has to make an entrance from a different side. This may muddle the dog and the best thing to do is to take her out for a run for a few minutes and start again as if it were a new action. Juno and Junia had brains that were so big that they could pick up any new thing in a few minutes. Junia even reasoned out

Jean with the author aged 23

Jyntee

Juno

Juno aged 6 months at her first show

Juno learning police-work training

Juno with Clark Gable

Juno with Odette Churchill

Juno has her elevenses

Junia aged 6 weeks waiting for a command

Junia learning to be a clever dog

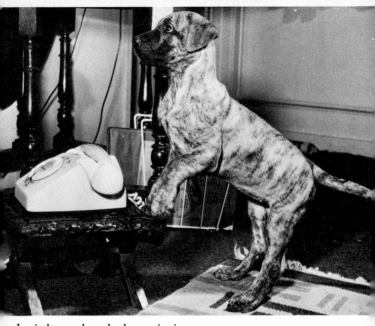

Junia hears the telephone ringing

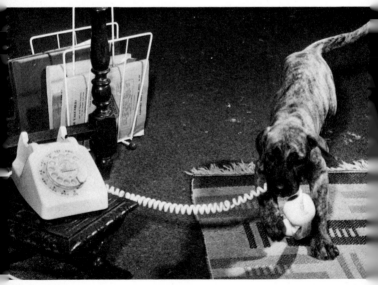

She answers it

o helps dry a newly born foal, Ducat; Florin, his mother, and Judith

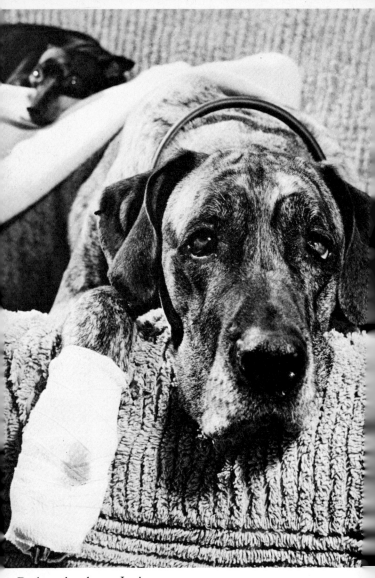

Broken glass lames Junia

Juno at play

Juno with Roger Moore

Eric Morecambe with Juno

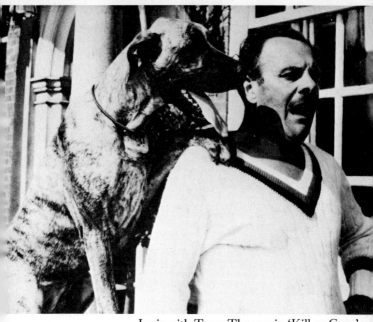

Junia with Terry Thomas in 'Kill or Cure'

Junia with Bruce Forsyth and Mini with Bob Monkhouse

Junia with Jonny Ross in 'Along the Way'

things for herself which helped the film. In one film she was acting with a child who was coming down a ladder. Junia was waiting at the bottom and as the child came within reaching distance of her head she licked the child's legs, which much improved the scene, but was entirely her own idea. At home one day my husband saw her trying to bring both her feeding bowl and Mini's at the same time, which of course was impossible. Then he saw her, entirely unaided, think the problem out. She put the two bowls inside each other and could then lift them up. After that we wondered what would happen if we put two bowls for her to bring which would not fit inside each other. This took her a very short time to solve. She put the two edges together and brought them to us. This I have on film. Junia seemed to pick up the thread of the story that was being filmed in an almost human way and lots of times her expression has added to the finished film. I suppose living so much with me and my family, with all that went on here, helped to make her that way. She and I were never parted for a single day in her whole life.

II

Wide Interest in Danes

I suppose dogs are the open sesame to friendships all over the world, certainly once a Dane owner always a Dane owner, and everyone who has ever owned one longs to bring out photographs and tell stories about their dog. I found this by my correspondence from all over the world from people who own Danes or who more often would like to own them. When I was in the States not long ago, I was staying at the Hilton Hotel in Pittsburgh and a man employed there came up to me and said he had heard I had had a Great Dane. He told me he bred them and had over thirty and would I like to go out and see them? How on earth he heard I'd a Dane when I only stayed one night there I don't know, possibly from the local Press. Unfortunately I hadn't time to go and see them, much as I should have liked to have done. For I am very interested in different types of Dane. I find it very difficult to assess

Danes' heads with their ears cropped. I suppose it makes them look alert but I think it makes them look too large and coarse in the head. What is wrong with an English Dane with beautifully small and correctly held ears?

Some years ago I went to Hamburg to do a television show on animals with Haggenbeck of circus fame. The show went out and was seen by a breeder of Danes at Ulm Donau in Germany. Herr Schlegel wrote to me and asked me if he could come to England and see me and talk Danes so I invited him to stay for the Dane of the Year show. I swotted up my German and he duly arrived. We went to the show and he was much impressed by what he saw there and gave me photos of his Danes and begged me to accept a present of one of his puppies. This of course I didn't want. I already had Juno and would never have wanted two Danes at the same time, especially as I always had a brindle and his were harlequins. I thought his harlequins quite nice in the photos I saw although I am not qualified to judge them, but they don't look to me any better than some of our dogs in this country. I found our conversation rather limited as he only had one reply to every subject I tried out and that was, 'Ja' or 'Nein'. Next year he again asked to come over, but I still never graduated to more than 'Ja' or 'Nein'! Either he was a man of few words or my German is worse than I thought it was. Perhaps amongst Dane owners telepathy is enough! Junia certainly liked him and that is good enough for me. He liked putting her to bed and kissing her goodnight.

Juno got letters from all over the world. Her films

83

were shown in Australia and she had quite a fan mail after that. My book, *Talking to Animals*, was published in the U.S.A. and I got a letter from a lady who asked me why the successor to Juno was called Junia, that was *her* name. I replied I thought I had invented the spelling and did not know it was anyone's name. I just liked it as a successor to Juno. Then another elderly person, also a lady, wrote to me from Scotland and said her name was Junia, where did I get the name from? Her father was a Methodist minister and got the name from the Bible where one of the prophets mentioned in the New Testament was called Junia. So I give up, there is nothing original in the whole wide world I think.

One gorgeous Valentine card addressed only 'Juno, England' was sent to Juno from the U.S.A. There was no delay, it was delivered right to our home without any remarks like 'Try . . . .'. I suppose Juno was seen so often on television and films that she was a household word.

I ran for some time a 'Juno Fan Club' through a magazine, and once a year had a huge children's party when we lived in the original Campions, which seventeenth-century house had a huge garden and could make a large gathering a very easy thing to organize. Juno loved these parties and went around welcoming the children as if she knew it was in her honour. We showed them films after tea and gave each one a Juno badge. Children so love to be connected with something famous like a dog. One child came all the way from Guernsey for the party.

We went to Guernsey one holiday with our children

and I gave a talk to the local Obedience Training Club and gave a demonstration with Juno, but we didn't meet any other Dane owners there, only cattle, but as I had a herd of Guernseys it made the holiday more interesting. Our landlady gave us fruit and custard twice a day for lunch and dinner at night every day we were there; my husband has never eaten custard since! But I must say the landlady was kind to Juno. She put an extra bed into our room especially for Juno which of course completely won my heart over to her, and there was nowhere Juno wasn't allowed to go.

One year I set out to raise money to make a film starring Junia which was to be donated to the Guide Dogs for the Blind. I thought, rather than buy a guide dog, which would eventually die, I could make a film that would go on the cinemas and bring in money for buying further guide dogs and the 16-mm print could go out with guide dog films from their headquarters and make an evening's entertainment for people. It is a comedy. I sent out hundreds of begging letters to everyone I knew and didn't know and was especially delighted to receive a very nice donation from a gentleman who lived in Beirut who also owned a Dane. I think this shows that Dane lovers everywhere have a mutual interest in the breed. The film is called 'Trouble with Junia', and many famous actors and actresses like Michael Balfour and Barbara Everest gave their services for a pittance to help such a good cause. It went on the cinemas and I hope will give enjoyment to people who borrow it from the Guide Dogs for the Blind in London for their social functions.

One of the things I ran to raise money for the making of the film was a luncheon at the Savoy Hotel in London, and guests of honour were Bruce Forsyth who owned a blue Great Dane, and Bob Monkhouse, an old friend of mine.

The luncheon was an enormous success, and Junia and Mini were given a place of honour lying on one of the tables in the centre of the function. Junia had to climb some stairs put for her to get on the table. As dogs aren't usually admitted to the Savoy I felt very honoured that mine should be so welcomed.

Another fund-raising idea of mine was to get Christmas cards made of a colour photo of Junia and the kittens on it, and sell it to the public by calling house to house. I sold 27,000 in this way. I soon got a sort of second sight about whether a house had anyone at home. Empty houses have a sort of aura which I picked up.

Once I had to mend a distraught woman's gas stove before she could attend to buying a packet of Christmas cards, another one's dog had a bit of training before the grateful owner bought my cards. Year after year I sold my own cards for the Guide Dogs for the Blind, and people often waited for me to call on them before buying any others. I really enjoyed meeting them all, and it certainly took off any surplus weight I had running up and down their drives.

Talking about dogs not being admitted to public places, I always remember a notice in Watford town hall which said: 'No dogs admitted except Juno'. I think she was everywhere accepted more as a personality than a dog.

She went to that town hall when the late Duchess of Kent visited the Printing Exhibition and proudly offered her paw to the Duchess when introduced, this brought the usual press publicity picture.

12

Holidays with a Dane

Holidays with a Dane are a problem. As I have already said, very few Danes thrive without their owners, and you have to decide on whether to find the sort of holiday you like with your dog, or risk leaving it in kennels hoping that it won't fret too much. The ideal of course is to have a friend or relative come to your home. My Danes would have fretted just the same if I had had this help, but it never arose as I can't remember anyone ever giving me this chance, and I doubt if I'd have enjoyed my holiday anyway worrying over my dog; I am made that way.

We had lovely holidays with Juno and Junia in Britain. One year we went to Torquay and there the manager of the big hotel we went to adored dogs, and the rules about keeping dogs in bedrooms only never applied to Juno. In return we entertained the guests one evening with two of Juno's films we took with us as I think evenings with young children, especially on a wet day, can be extremely boring on holiday. We always took one or two of our 16-mm films with us and Juno or Junia would entertain the other children in the hotel with their clever tricks. Very often the local newspaper heard that Juno was in their district and came and interviewed us. Once Juno did a piece of 'Keep Britain Tidy' for Torquay by being photographed picking up a piece of paper a visitor had just dropped and running with it and dropping it in the waste basket on the beach. Not only did it teach the visitors watching her performance, but the story was printed in the local paper and one of the national newspapers too.

When you own a film star dog, even on holiday, you have to keep up your publicity if your dog is to be famous. Juno and Junia were always willing to oblige and co-operate in any publicity I thought up, but were not always willing to do some of the silly things a few of the Press suggested. One I remember particularly was when a photographer asked if Juno could wink! She would however yawn on a signal from my hand, she would bark when I blinked my eyes, which is of course the way we get dogs to count, add or subtract in public, for no one is looking at the handler's eyes, they are watching intently for any signal by hand or foot.

People ask me how one trains a dog to do these things and of course the first thing to do is to see what the dog does naturally. Yawning, for example; every time she yawned naturally I used to say 'Yawnee' and give the hand signal of my two joined hands opening at the speed of her yawn and then give tremendous praise. In no time at all the dog realized by my tone of voice how happy it made me when she yawned. The words 'Clever girl' were music to my dogs, they so wanted to be praised and my excitement at their achievements was so easily transmitted. Lack of enthusiasm and excitement when dogs do well is one of my chief troubles in training owners. Few have this ability to transmit enthusiasm to their dogs, hence the dull eyes and indifferent work I meet with when dogs are first brought for training.

Another holiday we took was to Polzeath, where we went into digs, as the hotels didn't take dogs and the alternative would have been to leave the dogs (I had Juno and my daughter's little English Toy Terrier, Chica) in the car all night which was quite out of the question. When we arrived at the digs the rooms were so tiny we could hardly fit ourselves in, let alone Juno, and our landlady was like something out of a comedy on the films. It poured with rain nearly every day but rain or fine we were turned out of the house after breakfast, so we toured Cornwall from end to end trying to forget the rain. One Saturday, it was fine and I decided to run a 'Sports Afternoon' for dogs on Polzeath's huge beach. Every sport had to be run with dogs, like the potato race, thread the needle, etc.; and it is not easy to thread a needle with a dog's lead on your wrist unless it is very well trained. I'd collected old posters from newsagents and wrote on the back advertising the afternoon by sticking up posters all over the village and neighbouring villages. The proceeds were to go to the Guide Dogs for the Blind, a very favourite charity of mine. At 2.25 p.m. not a dog in sight and we thought our efforts had been in vain and that holiday-makers didn't like this sort of thing. Then all of a sudden it was like an army approaching, from every angle dogs and owners emerged. I should think we had at least 500 people and 60 or 70 dogs. The races were enormous fun and the spirit in which everyone entered the races was wonderful. Even the dogs seemed to love it although they did get rather pulled about on their leads, a few tripped up their owners which caused laughter, and by the end of the afternoon we had made quite a lot of money. I gave a demonstration of obedience training with Juno about half-time to give people a rest.

About fifteen months later I ran into a lady who had been at Polzeath and joined in that 'Dogs' Day' and she said she had enjoyed it so much that she had gone to Polzeath the next year and was very disappointed to find it was not put on again. This gave me an idea to run a 'Dogs' Day' here on the same lines some years later in aid of handicapped children and again this event was a tremendous success. It was filmed by Nationwide for television, and we raised over £350 for charity. It doesn't need a lot of organizing; I borrowed straw bales for people to sit on around the arena. A local ice-cream vendor paid for the ice-cream rights and a caterer came free to us for the right of selling refreshments. We ran it all day with ten separate events from races of every sort to simple things like a prize for the dog with the most tricks which produced a most marvellous wire-haired fox-terrier with a little girl. Unfortunately it started to rain and she went home without her prize which I always regretted. This 'Dogs' Day' idea is well worth copying for any event for charity, it is so easy to run. What was rather heartening was there wasn't a single fight amongst the 80 or more dogs who attended, and in the interval I offered to train any dog in five minutes in basic obedience and had a lot of dogs with faults offered to me as demonstration dogs. This was something I loved doing.

Then there was a holiday we had planned in the Emerald Isle which turned out to be a bit of a nightmare most of the time, but one incident pleased me. As we arrived in Larne the locals were just coming out of the cinema and as we were strolling along the street with Juno some children rushed up and said was that the dog in the film they had just seen, 'Trouble for Juno'? I glanced up at the title and sure enough her film was on. A lot of people came up and patted her and said how much they had enjoyed the film so that put me in a good mood. What didn't put me in a good mood was the astonishing number of dogs wandering in streets all over Ireland which seemed afflicted with mange, and my holiday was quite spoilt chasing away dogs from coming in contact with Juno for I know how infectious mange can be. We never repeated that holiday.

Juno and later Junia used to go everywhere I went. For years I lectured at women's luncheon clubs which necessitated a tremendous amount of travelling by train or by car and staying in hotels, some good, some utterly awful. One I remember was a motel that looked most luxurious but proved to be the coldest place on earth that winter's night for Juno. Our home was always kept at 68°F for comfortable warmth and I was terrified Juno would catch a chill, so spent the night getting up every hour to put another sixpence in the gas fire meter. That is what you do when you have a dog like Juno.

For twenty-one years I ran a farm and my Danes all treated cows and horses like other Great Danes, played with the calves and helped carry buckets to feed the horses. Juno lay by the fire once with two twin calves whose mother had gone down with milk fever and who had to be dried by me in front of a fire with the help of Juno who liked licking them. So it was nothing new for her to be bundled into a large pantechnicon when we went on holiday one summer with cows, children and dogs. I couldn't leave the cows because they were still in milk and nobody could hand-milk except me, even if I could have got help which I only once managed to do, so the only thing to do was to take all the animals except the horses with us, having rented an empty farmhouse for a month. We loved this holiday.

I was later on that year staying a night at a Westgate-on-Sea hotel and got talking as usual to the manager's wife, with Juno getting a lot of admiration, and told her how we'd love to bring the children to Westgate for a summer holiday but unfortunately it was impossible as we had cows. Her reply was: 'If your cows are as well behaved as Juno, you can bring them too, we'll empty the garage and they can have that!' I never took up that kind offer but I was a bit flattered that this kind lady should imagine I could train cows in the same way and up to the same standard as Juno was trained.

I did find the sun very trying for Juno on seaside holidays on a beach with no rocks for shade. Danes feel the heat quite a bit, so I always took two deck chairs and made a sort of house for mine with a towel on the top of the chairs forming shade, and I was always very careful to wash seawater out of the dog's coat as the salt can cause skin trouble. Juno loved the sea. Junia didn't like it so much. She had had a nasty experience of water when she was a youngster. I took her for a walk by the canal and she didn't realize what water was, so took a friendly flying leap into the canal to talk to a swan and couldn't get out easily due to the high wall. When we did heave her out she was shivering badly and got a terrible infection from the filth of the canal and had a temperature of 105°F. It took about ten days for her to recover, she was only four months old. She used to like paddling in the river but not swimming. I never made any of my Danes do anything they really didn't like doing. I think this is being fair to dogs, something I always insist on with dog owners.

One of the most disappointing of holiday plans was when the charity Cancer Research made arrangements to charter the QE2 for its maiden trial voyage. It was not going into any ports, just cruising in the Atlantic. Here at last was a chance to cruise with my dogs for they would not have to go into quarantine as long as the ship touched no land. I got in touch with the Ministry of Agriculture explaining how valuable my Junia and Mini (English Toy Terrier) were and what would happen if the ship broke down and had to go into a port and they were most sympathetic and we talked about lifting the dogs off by helicopter if this did happen. It was all very exciting. Arrangements had been made for us to have staterooms with an extra one for the dogs leading off mine. A grass lawn was to be laid for the dogs' toilet on deck and the treatment these dogs were to have was only equalled possibly by human stars. I had a very strong second sight feeling that this ship would never go on this trip. I am gifted with second sight and I thought I would make bets to this effect and insurance. I could achieve neither. I always thought William Hill had said that they would bet on anything but they turned me down flat. No insurance company would allow me to take out a policy covering cancellation of the trip. We were all ready to go, labels on our cases, dogs sensing something exciting was going to happen when the phone rang and we heard of the cancellation due to rotor trouble. Bang went the chance of a lifetime to enjoy a trip on that lovely ship and not be separated from my dogs. The publicity my dogs got for the project I am sure brought in money for Cancer Research, because as usual my Junia got national newspaper coverage with large photographs of the two dogs waiting with their suit-cases to go on the trip. What fun it would be if a ship were one day chartered for a dog-training cruise. I am sure it would be packed with people who could never go on a cruise with their dogs, and like this ship, it need not touch any port, just go for a cruise. There is an idea for some enterprising firm although I expect the Ministry of Agriculture would have a fit.

13

In Sickness and in Health

One of the saddest sights is to see a Dane ill. Their big
eyes are a picture of misery, for make no mistake, a
sick Dane puts on everything it can to get all the love
and sympathy when it feels ill. I suffered almost as
much as my dogs when my Danes were ill and having
done three years of vet training at college I knew just a
little about ills and probably worried more than most
people. My husband being a doctor was equally put
upon to use his brains to the utmost after I had said:
'Supposing Juno was a human being, what would you
do?' I had wonderful vets in my Danes' lives, Mrs
Cousens and Mr E. J. Heather, the first my local vet and
the other a famous vet who saw after the stadium
greyhounds amongst others in his practice at Oxford.
The first time I met him was when I was a young girl
with a very old pony and his kindness and sympathy
were outstanding as was his knowledge of animals. He

always seemed to have some idea up his sleeve that would rescue my animals from things no one else's animals used to suffer from.

Juno was a healthy dog on the whole. She came to me at three months old, rickety, terribly nervous but otherwise strong and healthy. Her rickets soon disappeared with proper treatment and her nerves followed suit very quickly. She was in her first beauty show at Seymour Hall at six months old, judged by an American judge who gave her first in every class she appeared in and wrote: 'This is the best Dane I have seen in years.' This in spite of the fact she must have lost points on 'flying ears' which she never grew out of. I didn't have her young enough to help them hang correctly but the way she used her ears was something that added to her character rather than taking away from her beauty. When she once won Best of Breed I nearly burst with pride. Her personality, huge bone size, beautiful brown eyes and a deep tiger marking made judges forget the flying ears. Luckily those ears were the correct size, not the huge elephant ears one sometimes comes across these days and which should be quickly bred out of the breed, as a Dane's expression is made by the use of its ears, which if too large and floppy lose all character.

Junia was a different kettle of fish. We nicknamed her 'the antibiotic queen' for she always had something to fight. At her first heat she passed a cupful of pus and had to have antibiotics to clear that up. At the same time she had intermittent diarrhoea and hot burning ears. Then we discovered this was all due to an *Escherichia coli* infection. It is a very common thing in Danes and should be recognized when the puppy does not put on weight and remains 'herring gutted' in spite of everything one can do. Luckily we tried chloromycetin on her and it knocked this infection flat and Junia thrived. I found a home-made sponge cake was the one thing that put weight on Junia. Every day without fail I made one with three eggs, their weight in butter and sugar, and she had it for her supper. An old lady in the country told me to do this and it certainly worked for Junia became as beautiful as any Dane should be, but it took time and worried me a lot.

I always had a sofa in both sitting-rooms for all my Danes as they should never lie on the floor. Not only are they then out of the way with their enormous bodies but one doesn't tread in error on their feet or trip over them when running to the phone. Old sofas can usually be bought for a few pounds at furniture sales and if the dog has her own blankets which then go with her in the car or to hotels, or in my Danes' case to a film studio, she is always happy. The blankets can be washed easily and she will not smell. All my Danes have had frequent baths but didn't need a lot of grooming for people stroked and patted them all the time which produces a lovely shine on a dog's coat. In the Argentine where I had Jean she would get hosed every day in summer for the heat was excessive, sometimes 110°F in the shade, but she seemed to stand the heat quite well.

England may be a country fit for heroes to live in, but it certainly isn't a country fit for dogs to play in, thanks to litter louts. Four times in twelve months Junia was badly cut by broken glass in the open spaces of Hertfordshire. Once on a golf course, twice in different woods and once on Chorleywood Common. In each case she was galloping and having a wonderful time, as only a young healthy dog of two years old can have when free. The third time she severed an artery in her front paw, the wound gouged out a deep piece of the pad besides cutting the paw in four other places. Had I not had a little veterinary knowledge and known how to stop the bleeding I might have lost my dog. As it was, the wounds could not be stitched, as the stitches wouldn't have held – the pads were too spongy – and Junia had to be bandaged and stay on the lead for four months. Luckily it was winter and Junia was not making a film at the time. Every time she wanted to go and relieve herself in the garden I had to put a plastic bag on her paw over the bandages to keep them dry. Eventually the wound healed and I took her to a small wood where I didn't think any picnickers would have left their hateful broken bottles. Freed, Junia behaved like a wild horse racing over the high bracken in great big jumps, wild with joy at being free again. Her joy was short-lived. Suddenly she stopped galloping and stood still with ears laid flat against her head, holding up one front paw. Once again she had severely cut the other front paw on glass.

This time it appeared to be a broken milk bottle that had been fired at by boys with a rifle, and was at the base of a big tree. Poor Junia was back in bandages, and on the lead when she went out. Never could I free her again without protection against litter louts and their lethal left-behinds. I found that the quickest way to treat pad wounds was to soak the foot thoroughly in peroxide and then apply a little round pad of cotton wool soaked in some antibiotic like aureomycin and then build up protection for this pad with 'New Skin'. I used to apply it over the cotton wool and when dry apply another layer, always leaving a hollow in the middle so that the wound was never actually pressed upon. Junia seemed to be able to walk without discomfort, but I decided to try and buy some boots for her. First of all I approached all the big stores to see if boots were made for dogs and found that waterproof boots for Poodles, etc., were easily bought but when it came to glassproof, waterproof boots for a ten-stone Great Dane it was a very different thing. The design of such things was a very skilled matter, and no one had ever perfected one.

Firstly I had to have plaster casts made of her feet. To do this she had to be lifted on to a bench and stand absolutely still for a long period whilst the plaster dried, then a cast was made from that. Next we had to find a leather soft enough for her to wear without rubbing her toes when in movement. To help me I enlisted the help of a man who makes appliances for human patients at a big London hospital and a Polish bootmaker of surgical boots in Star Street, Paddington. We found a wonderfully soft kid which, lined with sheepskin, could not possibly rub. But this of course would not prevent glass cutting her foot through the kid if she trod on razor-like broken bottles. The answer was to use a plastic that was so strong you could not pierce it with a razor blade. The boots were made to the shape of the cast and I thought all would be well. It took ten seconds for her to throw them off her feet.

The tremendous impetus caused by her galloping at about twenty-five miles per hour soon saw to that. The fastening by a strap was useless. Not only that, the dog could not hold herself upright as the soles of the boots became slippery. She had been used to using her toenails and pads to stop and turn with. So we abandoned the straps and zip-fasteners and made the opening of the boot at the rear with a tongue, then used the self-adhesive fastening 'Velcro' which only sticks to itself and can be unstuck in a second and stuck again as often as you wish without any sticking to the person or dog in contact with it. This was a great step forward, but we still had to do something about her turning and falling down due to lack of pads.

Once again we took impressions of her pads and stuck flexible rubber pads exactly like her own feet on to the bottoms of the boots. At last she could gallop without losing the boots, and turn without losing her balance. Junia then could carry on her exercise without apparent discomfort. She would nearly always do this injury just as she was in the middle of a film or television commitment, so after she did it three times I had to give up taking her to the woods whilst working. Then one day I decided to give her a treat and take her to the woods; the boot failed her, she got it off and cut a tendon in half in her foot; from that day to her end, one toe was flat. It healed but never recovered its proper bunched-up look and never again was Junia free in the woods. Dull walks by the river never compensated for freedom to chase things and if I did go to the woods she was kept on a lead.

Until the British Isles educates its population so

that they take their litter home, and the open spaces are cleaned up and free from broken glass and tins, dogs cannot enjoy their heritage safely, and film star dogs must wear boots, which only give partial protection, or stay on the lead always.

Poor Junia also suffered from slipped discs. She was always leaping about and enjoying life so much that a sudden turn would slip a disc. Luckily I learnt to manipulate her discs and she would come up to me with a hanging head and an expression which said: 'Missus, I've done it again.' I manipulated her back and immediately she would leap about, telling me as best she could, 'Thank you, I'm all right.' Nothing she did ever stopped her enjoyment of life and her working in films and television which was her life. If only people knew how dogs love working they would try and find some sort of work for their dogs to do. It sharpens the brain, brings out the best in a dog, and the eagerness to do something clever is so obvious that anyone who thinks a working dog has a hard life should watch a trained dog enjoy itself being clever. That is of course if it is trained kindly, handled sympathetically and never allowed to be overworked.

14

Owning a Dane

To own a Great Dane is a privilege, a responsibility and an experience never to be quite repeated, in my opinion, with any other breed of dog. Danes seem to have an inherent love for their owners and the willingness to please and receive love more than any other dog I've met, with perhaps the exception of an Alsatian, but I know everyone thinks this about their own dog.

Some people get a Great Dane from the feeling of 'oneupmanship' or just sheer vanity, because, make no mistake, no one passes a Great Dane without looking, and this looking adds to the pride of ownership if the dog is well behaved, well groomed and beautiful to look at. Alas, not all Great Danes are like this these days; there are far too many 'herring-gutted' ones which, interpreted, means their bodies shrink upward under the tummy and give them a greyhound look which is not glamorous at all. This often comes from an inborn infection from the dam. If this is the case, no amount of food from a desperate owner will rectify it, only correct veterinary treatment. So many people buy a Dane and listen to the tales of what enormous amounts of food they will need, which precludes many a Dane from getting a really loving home, and which has been proved time and time again to be utterly wrong. Any dog can eat the owner out of house and home and as the old saying goes, 'What goes in one end must come out the other', but in the case of a Dane they thrive on a much smaller amount of food when adult and therefore do not cost so much to keep as is generally believed; but it must be the right food. When people think about having a Dane they imagine it is a great strong dog able to live outside in all weathers and guard the premises, with its huge size and deep-throated barking that would be terrifying to burglars. What the owners often don't know is that they are often quite difficult dogs to rear to their full size and beauty.

However you rear a Dane you can't get features that it doesn't possess from its hereditary factors, but you can improve on some, for example ear carriage, by constantly encouraging the ears, after teething is completed, to go forward into the correct position which is done by pushing them forward eliminating the wrong crease some ears have. You can train the puppy to be interested in everything and therefore develop the lovely neck and ear carriage so essential to Dane character and looks.

If I were a Great Dane breeder I would think very

carefully before I sold a puppy to any person not having previously successfully owned or known a Dane. I would find out if they realized Danes break their hearts if left alone for long periods, if put into boarding kennels or if allowed to roam alone. They only become intelligent, and loving, faithful pets if talked to, trained and played with from the moment they enter the home. They have to have an enormous amount of rest and sleep when tiny to give the body the chance to double its size in a few weeks and to allow the enormous bones to develop correctly. It is quite essential in my opinion to have an indoor kennel, either home-made or bought, to give to the Dane its own special place where nobody disturbs it and where it can sleep much of the day away when a tiny puppy. I have always if possible had my Dane puppies at six weeks old. Mrs Davies of Oldmanor fame said to me I was one of the few people she would let a puppy of this age go to, as many buyers don't realize the needs of a puppy of this age. I think having my puppy at this age made an enormous difference to its intelligence and well-being.

Warmth is absolutely vital to Dane puppies and my husband made an indoor kennel for mine which could be added to in height as my puppy grew every few weeks, but the back of the kennel was made of a wire netting so that it was placed against the radiator in the winter months when I bought her, and she then slept all night and never soiled her kennel which I think must be almost a record.

Great Danes are naturally clean; given the chance to relieve themselves and trained to do so on command, they will never soil the house. So many newcomers to owning a Dane imagine it is one of the chores of owning a puppy to clean up after it. This is definitely not so. If you choose the place you wish your puppy to use outside and give it the same command and abundant praise when it relieves itself on your command, that puppy will never be anything but clean. Danes possibly more than many other dogs adore praise, you will only get an intelligent dog if you talk to it, using a wide range of tones of voice, which is so easily interpreted by a puppy willing and interested in learning what you are saying. It is rather like a young child who is perpetually asking why and what. The expression on a puppy's face as you use different tones of voice tells you instantly whether you are an owner worth listening to or merely an owner.

It is most important before having a Dane to find out the reactions of the rest of your family to having a big dog like this, and a dog with the character that is so loving that holidays abroad have often to be ruled out unless someone it loves and knows is left with it. I stayed with my Danes Juno and Junia for twenty-one years, only once going abroad. The general manager at Heathrow once came up to me as I waved goodbye to my family on a plane for an overseas holiday and said: 'Why is it we see you and your dog always waving goodbye, never going on a plane?' and I pointed to my dog with me and told him: 'If you own a Dane you never let it down.' My family agreed and understood that, and most of our holidays were spent in Britain. I remember once we were going to Ireland from Stranraer with the car and the schedule for planes was decidedly vague, so after waiting about an hour I said to the manager: 'My dog is bored! When on earth are we getting a plane?' His response was to call to a pilot standing near by: 'Come over, Michael, and take the lady over. Her dog is bored and we can't have that', and with that we were ushered to a waiting plane and taken over by ourselves. What happened to other passengers I just don't know. Great Danes have this effect on people. Nobody can help wanting to stroke them unless they are dog haters. The only person I ever met who was like this was Marlene Dietrich who had to stand to be photographed with my two dogs, a Dane and an English Toy Terrier, for a charitable affair for the blind, and she shrunk from Juno saying: 'All dogs smell.' This infuriated me because if ever a dog was beautifully clean and without smell it was my Juno with whom she was to be photographed. Luckily the resulting photo did not visibly show her apparent dislike of dogs.

Actually, in my life with Danes, I've found it far more difficult to put up with the affection for my dogs from people than the opposite. I have often been terribly sorry for them with the amount of patting, kissing, etc., they have had to put up with from utter strangers for whom they cared nothing, for a Dane is a one-man or one-woman dog and outsiders mean nothing but boredom for a beloved Dane. But my dogs did a vast amount for charity. Juno used to collect an average of £7 an hour standing with her boxes for blind babies in Hamley's doorway in London. No one could pass her magnificence, and often if anyone stopped but didn't put money in, the look she gave them was almost human.

15

The Family Dog

I get asked a number of times in a year about a family
with young children having a Dane and my answer is
always the same: Danes are as a general rule the
gentlest of dogs and make ideal family pets. By and
large they are extremely careful where they tread and
how they play with very young children. They are
patience itself when it comes to having their ears
pulled, their backs climbed over, and their bones taken
away from them by children. But like any breed there
are the good ones and the not so good ones. Danes
that rush about the house, get up and leap towards the
door when they hear anyone approach are likely to
have accidents in the home. An excitable Dane is far
too confined in a home not to cause some kind of
accident or disturbance at one time or another. If a
baby gets trodden on by a Dane's paw it certainly
hurts it, and may make the child frightened of dogs

for some time. I had Juno and Jyntee when my children were young, and never once did anything like this happen, for the dogs were trained (or never needed training) to be the perfect companions to my children.

Juno played Red Indians in the garden. She even learnt to play French cricket, which Pathé Pictorial filmed for their news magazine in the cinema. No one believed a dog could actually hold a tennis racket, hit a tennis ball bowled to her and run to the stumps as does a human being, but Juno just loved this sort of thing. I even taught her to blow bubbles with a pipe. Some people think teaching dogs 'tricks' as they call them is cruel. I know for a fact dogs love doing anything you can teach them in a household, especially where children are concerned. Therefore my dogs' lives as film and television stars were only a continuation of what they loved doing in the home. But the praise they received made that life good for them, and often in the studios the dog would go around, tail wagging madly, to everyone who told her what a clever dog she was. She posed for photographs but would get impatient if the photographer failed to get the correct photo in about six takes. One almost felt she would have liked to do the job herself properly.

Children with a Dane in the home have to learn to respect its rights. My Dane always had her own sofa to lie on and nobody was ever allowed to touch her when on that sofa. That was the place she had peace and quiet to sleep. If they wanted her for any reason she had to be called off it, and she was then amenable to doing anything anyone wanted. But again she was not asked to do things when she'd done enough for one day. No child of mine was ever allowed to take either Juno or Junia out by him or herself. I think this is a very wise precaution with a Dane. It isn't what your Dane will do, it is what other people's dogs will do. Quite a few times in my life I have encountered other people's horrible dogs who have attacked my dog without any cause whatsoever. Once when Juno was sitting quietly in the post office a great Boxer dog came in and instantly, being off the lead, attacked her viciously. She never retaliated for she was trained not to, and I fought for her survival against this horrible dog. Its owner came in as I was in the middle of pulling it off my dog. He had a terrible job holding it, and I passed out on the floor. So you see what a danger it could be if an incident like this had happened with a child in charge.

Another time I was walking with Junia in our woods and an Alsatian sprang out of the bracken, fixed its teeth into her back, tearing her skin quite deeply. She bore the scar for the rest of her life. This particular Alsatian was well known to the police for this behaviour but the owner still risked injuring someone else's dog by allowing it freedom in the woods on walks. Actually the owner and I came to an agreement whereby I would tie a piece of red ribbon to a tree when I had Junia in the woods. She explained to me that there was nowhere she could ever let this dog off where it would not be a danger, but was adamant that it had to be free. I warned her about injuring other people's dogs, but she wouldn't take a warning. The dog eventually severely injured a tiny dog and I don't know what happened.

Recently an acquaintance of mine, after I'd warned her to have her Dane castrated as it was getting nasty with other dogs, sent her twelve-year-old son out with the dog for its evening walk just around the block with no lead on. The dog met an enemy Boxer and the two had the most almighty fight. The Dane nearly killed the Boxer who had forty-eight stitches in its body and the son got badly bitten by his own dog in trying to separate them. A court case ensued and the whole family was miserable, because how can they ever let that dog off again safely? They are sure to have had an order to keep the dog under control and no child could do this.

Children love training Danes, but I feel the parents should do the initial jerks on the choke chain which are so essential to happy obedience. I train many youngsters with their dogs of all breeds. The youngest I ever had was six and she knocked spots off her parents who were on my training course with two of their other dogs. Her voice was just the right tone, her signals impeccable and the fun she gave the dog as she praised it was just right. My own daughter Judith trained her little English Toy Terrier when she was six, and often beat Alsatians in the obedience ring with this little 6-lb dog. The dog must be within the strength of the child handler and this means a young three-months-old Dane. When older they get too heavy for a small child to handle.

No child should in my opinion be allowed to ride on a Dane's back. Danes are not as strong as they look in the back. I have known quite a few with upper dorsal slipped discs and even more with lumbar discs caused by people pressing their backs to make them sit or lie down. I never allow anyone to press any dog to the sit. I make them put the second finger of the left hand in the offside thigh of the dog with the thumb lightly over the back, but never pressing on it, and pulling the dog's quarters back into the sit with a sort of pincer movement. The biggest dog has to sit with a minimum amount of effort on the handler's part with this action. You can't fight a large Dane; you have to use dog ju-jitsu and know what puts it off balance. If you bungle in these exercises the dog is inclined to retaliate with a bite, and once a dog does this it is a very backward step. If you bungle any exercise by mistake, remember a gentle slow tickle on the dog's chest between its front legs produces a calm and happy dog. Don't try to fight or ever hit a dog that bites. It just makes things worse. Next time you can do the exercise with a muzzle on the dog if it really bites, then it has to obey and cannot hurt you. A Dane remembers who is master very quickly, and I have seldom had to muzzle any dog for more than a few minutes.

Jealousy very very rarely occurs in Danes, but be sure to introduce a new baby to a Dane as soon as possible, and do not push it away. Don't under any circumstances let it lick the baby, but to be friends it must be allowed to sniff it. Show no anxiety for the baby's safety or health and the dog will accept it at once. Fear is the one thing that could cause trouble if shown by the parents, so relax.

To get the right family friendship between the Dane in the home and the children, I think it a very good thing to let the children groom the dog, help bath the dog and feed it sometimes under supervision, and certainly games with the children can be the highlight of the day. Jyntee adored playing hide-and-seek in our large garden, and even though she knew where the children had hidden by their scent, she used to look in all sorts of places to pretend she didn't know. Danes have very good noses. Juno found my contact lens in gravel when I lost it one day.

Danes love work to do. If you think they only need to be bought, fed and exercised you are utterly wrong. They must join in everything you do and you would be wrong to exclude them from helping where helping is possible. Start by training your puppy to do ordinary basic obedience like sit, stay, heel, wait, down, and carry, and you've got a basis for helping you. Danes in particular like carrying things. My nine-weeks-old Junia would carry my shopping basket, carry her lead, fetch her feeding bowl, open the dining-room cupboard and fetch her own biscuits, bark as a request for one, shut the door, lift off the ringing telephone and fetch me by barking to come and answer it, take the morning paper upstairs. These were only a few of the things she would eventually do when she became a famous film star. I made a film of her doing all these things because people possibly might not believe what a nine-weeks-old puppy could do and what is more do it with shining eyes and an obvious enjoyment in being clever. I think more people should see this film and realize the capabilities of a Dane.

So many people leave puppies much too long without teaching them things, they are then just dogs, not almost human as most Danes become with the proper treatment and teaching. A Dane must be a full member of the family; it has earned its right to be this over generations of contact with humans, and it is waiting for the right owner to blossom to the full. A nasty Dane is quite out of keeping with the Dane character, yet today there are some nasty Danes. I think by seeing my two Danes in films and television so much, people thought Danes naturally did all the things mine did, and bought one without realizing that I was extremely careful what sort of Dane I bought, how I reared it, how I talked to it and trained it. My Danes were born right, but were made right too.

16

Buying a Dane

Having decided that the dog you wish to own is a Great Dane, think and think wisely before going and buying one on the spur of the moment. First of all work out who is going to see after it, who is going, for the first few days in your home, to take it out to relieve itself about every two hours, wet or fine, cold or hot, who is going to get up early in the morning so it doesn't have to soil its sleeping quarters because of a lazy owner; who is going to prepare its food and see that it is fed at regular hours, which is absolutely vital in the successful rearing of a Dane puppy. They are not big eaters but as small puppies have to have five meals a day at regular intervals in the right amounts, so that the body can digest these meals and make the best of them in the development of the puppy. Good meat, good brown bread or meal, milk, and supplementary vitamins and calcium, trace elements, and minerals to ensure proper growth and development all cost money. If it is winter it is advisable to have a waterproof coat for the puppy so that biting winds and rain do not deter it from relieving itself in discomfort which often produces failure, as the puppy's only thought is to rush back into the warmth of the home. Coats can be made to measure by the Sandon Saddlery Co. with the dog's name in the corner like a race-horse's rug.

What sort of indoor kennel will you have? Have you someone who will make one? A box or basket is not suitable for a Dane puppy. I turned the cupboard under the stairs into my Dane's first home as the heating pipes went under the floor and it was very cosy. I simply took off the door and put a Penfold wire door on instead, made by my very handy husband. She could hear all that went on in the house and was very happy, until her bigger kennel in my study became her home. Later the sides and top were taken off and it was her permanent bed with one of my children's old cot mattresses as the bedding. This was just the right size for a Dane, so look out for one from a friend if you haven't got one. This size often fits very nicely into the back of an estate car for the Dane to ride on in comfort too. I am always appalled at people who put dogs in the back of an estate car on just a blanket. I'd like them to ride on such an uncomfortable and hard surface for miles, yet dogs have to put up with this very often. And whilst on the subject of cars, be sure to keep a cushion in the car so that you can put it on the ground for the Dane to jump on to. Danes slip their discs or injure their shoulders quite easily when jumping from a height, and it is vital to prevent this happening. I used to use an old cushion from a disused armchair and kept it in the car. It was resilient to the weight of my dog and it helped her jump into the car, too, which was quite a height for a puppy.

Now you must turn to where you are going to buy a Dane. What colour you are going to choose, what sex you are going to have and above all where will you get the right Dane temperament from, for a vicious or bad-tempered Dane is something I would not like to own, especially when an adult Great Dane dog can be over 36 inches in height and a big bitch often up to 36 inches in height. Breeders have in recent years been breeding dogs bigger and bigger until in my opinion they are too long on the leg and too big for many households. It isn't the actual size of a Dane you should seriously consider, it is the all round conformation, and colour particularly. The colour of the eyes matters to me a lot. Brown eyes are found in all colours with the exception of harlequins or blues, an attribute that I value highly. All my life I've known that dark-eyed dogs are in some way kinder and more intelligent than light-eyed dogs. The expression is more easily able to be defined in a dark-eyed dog. A yellow-eyed dog can show little change of depth, and as the trainer I am, I learn to gauge the mood of a dog by the expression in the eye. Naturally if you wish to own a harlequin or a blue Dane, their eyes are mostly light so this warning doesn't apply.

The colour of the dog you choose must really appeal to you, and if possible be well inside the standard set by the Kennel Club if you wish to show the dog. For example, white on a Dane with the exception of a harlequin is frowned upon, yet today one sees many dogs with white paws or even black hairs on a fawn. One meets poor-coloured brindles, pale fawns, and slightly rust-coloured blacks. This of course doesn't matter if you only want a pet dog, but if you want to show you may be disillusioned with what the judge reports. I always think if you do get the chance to have a good dog it costs no more to keep, although it costs more to buy in the first place. I always chose a brindle with a deep fawn coat under the stripes which closely resembled tiger markings and are much admired. If you get one of these you have reason to be very proud as they need looking for.

I think a future Dane owner should go to shows and round to many breeders before buying a puppy, see the parents of the puppies for temperament and choose from friendly parents. Sharp dogs may appear to be good guards, but in Danes you hardly need to think about guarding your home. This is an in-born trait in Danes and their bark is invaluable in warding off unwelcome intruders.

Never choose the small shy puppy that won't come out and talk to a visitor; it is likely to be a nervous adult, and need special care and training. Breeders should try to get people at an early age to talk to their puppies. Human contact is essential from an early age if a non-shy and friendly adult is to be achieved. The Kennel Club, Clarges Street, London W1, will give addresses of breeders. There are many Great Dane clubs who will also be willing to give advice if people join the clubs. If possible buy a puppy about eight to ten weeks old, it is seldom satisfactory to buy an older puppy, say five months, because it has lived in kennels, has not been able to be house-trained, has not had the training to understand human ways and talk and therefore has to start at an age when one would expect the puppy to have been nearly fully trained.

Don't imagine you can buy a Dane and turn it out in a garden all day and then expect it to be intelligent, clean and obedient. I hate gardens for dogs unless the owner is with the dog. What is a poor dog to do in a garden? Dig it up? This produces a scolding. Play hide-and-seek in the shrubbery, knocking the shrubs flying? This is frowned upon. Eat stones? Something most Danes do in growing up. We call it the 'stone age' and it usually means the dog lacks minerals and is trying to get these from stones. Give Vionate as an additive to its diet, this usually stops this vice. There is nothing to hunt in your garden. In the summer a rest in the sun is appreciated and helps the storing up of vitamin D in the body, but in winter a garden just makes dogs scatty with nothing to do. Your home with you is the place for a Dane, the place they love most of all.

I once put a pedometer on my leg and carried out my ordinary chores and found that my Dane having followed me around had done six miles of walking, so whoever says Danes can't live in small houses or flats is wrong providing they have the owner with them to follow about and if they go for proper exercise. A Dane is happy wherever its owner chooses to live.

A well-trained Dane does not knock things off tables. They are as careful of your china as they are of your tiny children. A Dane is thoughtful for the family. Only if you've noticed a Dane gently stepping around things, light as a feather, do you realize how intelligent these dogs can be, and I say 'can' for some are stupid wild creatures quite unsuitable for a small home or even a big one with anything breakable about. But this is not the Dane's fault. It is the owner's fault. Danes are made or marred, like children, by those they belong to. As a breed they are superb at picking up atmosphere and abiding by rules, but some people these days are unfit to own Danes. Once you have chosen the Dane you want, let it be imprinted on your mind that this is for life, for better or for worse, you can't just get rid of a Dane when the mood changes and you find owning a dog a bind or a tie. Danes break their hearts if deserted by their owners. They often become unmanageable with fear and nerves, and end up by being put to sleep or found a so-called good home, which may not last very long. For make no mistake, any 'second-hand' dog has certain factors built into its early training which need love and understanding to change, and owners find this re-educating tedious. I myself had two of the most wonderful Danes in my life second-hand, my first Dane, Jean, and my second Dane, Jyntee. I never want more faithful friends.

17

Your New Dane

For the purpose of this chapter I am going to assume
you have bought a puppy, not adopted an older dog or
bought one from a lost dogs' home.

You will, I presume, go and fetch the puppy you
have chosen when it is old enough to go to a new
home. It would be jeopardizing its future if it were
sent by train, the delays and uncertainties of this mode
of transport would not be worth risking.

Take with you a blanket so the puppy can lie on
someone's lap; take a baby's bib or piece of sheeting so
that if the puppy dribbles and is car sick no harm will
be done. Puppies and dogs are only car sick because of
the imbalance of the semi-circular canals in the ears,
therefore eliminate this as much as possible on the
puppy's first trip in a car by keeping it on someone's
lap, preferably in the back seat of the car. For ever the
puppy must learn the back seat is his, not the front

seat where any dog is a risk to the driver and itself if
an accident occurs, or even if an accident doesn't occur
by its involuntary or even voluntary fidgeting. The
word 'back' must be said in a tone of voice not to be
argued with, and if necessary as the puppy gets bigger
a piece of string can be run between the two back
doors and the puppy anchored to this by a string or
short piece of lead so it can't jump forward. It must
from the very first be taught to lie down and stay
down. As a tiny puppy a very gentle tickling of the
chest soothes and makes it sleepy. Very gentle stroking
right from the head to the tail and gentle pressure if it
tries to stand up ensures a peaceful journey. Bad
drivers make dogs car sick. The bad changing of gears,
the sudden acceleration or stopping of a bad driver
who doesn't gauge his distances or has slow reactions
are very prone to make dogs sick in cars. A steady
smooth gear change, a gentle acceleration and avoiding
sudden stops as lights change give the dog or puppy
confidence. Once a dog travels in a car without being
sick it is unlikely to be sick in the future. If it is, leave
the puppy in the car while it is stationary outside the
home for at least an hour a day, with its own blanket
for company and preferably after a meal when it will
be naturally sleepy. For a dog that can relax and sleep
in the vehicle is unlikely to be sick. If it barks and
stands up and won't relax, try going back very crossly
and put it in the down position and tell it to stay. This
is where sensible early obedience training helps. If the
puppy continues to get up on four feet and creates a
noise in the car, put a choke chain on it on a length of
string and run it under the safety-belt anchorage, and

face the road ahead of you gently pulling the string attached to the collar which runs under the seat belt anchorage. This applies downward pressure on the dog's neck and it has to lie down; once down the dog will not bark and should not be sick. It will not associate the downward pull with the owner, but the owner must repeat the command 'down' until the puppy obeys. I do not suggest this should be done by the driver but by a passenger. By not looking at the puppy, it does not connect the correction with the owner, and therefore obeys from the pressure.

Always be sure to let the puppy relieve itself before a car journey. Travelling excites a puppy and when excited the natural reaction is to urinate. Junia, my Dane, was amazing. When adult she would travel all over the country with me and when I thought she needed to relieve herself I would stop the car and take her out. Although she had only once been at that spot, if ever I passed that way again, be it 500 miles from where I lived, Junia would get up and look out ready to be allowed to get out once again at the same spot, although a few minutes earlier she might have been asleep. How dogs know these things is beyond me. Dog brains and instincts, telepathy and understanding are past human understanding and knowledge. I always swear my Junia was reincarnated from my Juno, as she never had to be taught anything and knew exactly what actions to do from a tiny puppy of six weeks old. Her expressions, her reactions to my thoughts were identical to Juno's as were Juno's to Jyntee's before her. I am not a believer in this normally, but it almost seemed possible. I wonder what other people have experienced.

Once the journey home has been achieved the puppy should have a meal and be taken with a command to relieve itself to the spot he or she is to use for a toilet in future, and then be put to bed in the indoor kennel, or whatever has been prepared. No pleadings from younger members of the family should be listened to to play with the puppy, for as a tiny puppy she must at all costs have a sleep and rest, nor must she or he be carried about, squeezed or dropped as is sometimes the prerogative of children, who mean to be loving. When the puppy has had its food and a sleep, it can then be allowed out if it has again relieved itself, for a short play with the children or admiration from grown-ups. Its name should be used often. Naming a dog correctly is vital; the name should be easily pronounced and audible from a distance; it should conjure up the dog's looks and character, for dogs seem to grow like their names. It should not end in S because this takes away from the sound when calling the dog. So few people have good voices when calling their dogs and often blame the dog for not coming when called when in reality the dog has not heard the call when engaged on doggy pursuits. An I or a T are excellent for name endings; an M as in Sam is good; the shorter the name the easier to call. If you give a dog a long name it could be out of hearing before you have finished calling the name, which would then be the owner's fault if the dog did not respond.

I recommend training a puppy with a dog whistle at the same time as you give the dog its name and command; for example, 'Juni come', and give a blow on the whistle. If you've watched sheepdog trials you will see how dogs respond to the shepherd's whistle even though the dog is a long way off. I was once asked, if there were two people in the same area with dog whistles, to whom would the dog go? My reply is, a whistle tone is made by the owner according to the amount of breath used, and it is most unlikely that two strangers would be using the same amount of breath at the same moment, so I think it is a million to one chance that your dog would go to someone else. It would soon get disillusioned if the stranger did what I always hope strangers will do to any dog I am training, send it back to me or any other owner with a very cross voice. People who talk to other people's dogs and make a fuss of them when they are being called by the owner are selfish, unthinking, vain creatures who preen themselves thinking they are popular with dogs, forgetting that not returning to an owner on command could one day cause an accident, fight or just getting lost. I once asked a lady with a dog lead in her hand to give Junia a flick with it as she was interested in sniffing this stranger and not obeying my command. The answer I got was: 'Oh, she is so beautiful I couldn't smack her.' My reply was: 'She may be beautiful now but would not be so beautiful run over if she disobeyed me.' Owners must *never* smack their dogs for not coming when called, so one is pretty helpless out on a country walk. It sometimes takes over an hour to catch a wilful dog, that is why in my school I take dogs into fields and send them back to their owners with a flick of a soft lead in my hand, and ask all the other pupils to do the same. The dog learns where he is going to get a welcome from the owner and a nasty scolding voice and a possible flick with a lead from anyone else. It works. That is why a training school held in a hall is not always effective for this naughty behaviour of not coming when called. Dogs are clever, they know when they are in a hall and unable to thwart the owner, but it is a very different matter when they are free in a park and are interested in other dogs or smells. I tell my owners they are 'second fiddle to a smell' which is not very complimentary. I don't recommend titbits, not all dogs want them and they soon catch on that this is a trick and become cunning. Proper obedience training from the moment they come to the home, tremendous love when they come and if possible help from someone to send them back is the answer.

It is vital when a puppy comes to your home to watch its motions. If they are solid, a good colour and not more than two or three a day then the puppy is well, but a change of home and food, although the breeder has possibly given you a diet sheet, often produces an upset tummy. If the motion is bright yellow and runny consult a vet, for the puppy may have a chill, may be riddled with worms, although it should have been wormed twice before it came to you, and should be wormed again within a short time. Very occasionally a puppy has tapeworms and you will see the square segments in the motion. Take immediate action with the co-operation of your vet if you see these, they are dangerous to humans, and the puppy will never thrive.

Be sure to put a tiny round sewn-in-the-centre collar on the puppy and pay no attention to scratching. I never understand people who take dogs' collars off in the house or at night as if the dog was undressing for bed; it is quite unnecessary. The name and address should always be on the collar which must be made larger very often. I am often shocked by the tightness of puppies' collars that come to me. There is nothing that makes a puppy bite quicker than to be held by a too-tight collar. Not only is it painful but bad for its neck. Collars for Danes need renewing very often; the rate of growth is phenomenal. The photo shows my Junia at eight weeks. When she came to me at six weeks she crawled easily under the tiny English Toy Terrier.

18

Feeding a Dane

First and foremost the correct feeding of a Dane is absolutely vital for its growth. I do not believe as some people do that a Dane can be reared for next to nothing. I genuinely believe you have to have the means to buy the right food or your Dane will suffer in its initial growth.

I read recently that a breeder suggested a Dane could be fed for £3 a week in 1976; this I just don't believe if you feed it on the right nourishing food, provide the supplementary food essential to healthy growth of body and bone, and give the Dane the shiny coat, the bright eye and health which denote a properly reared one. Many people think that to give the puppy vast quantities of food ensures that it will grow into a big healthy dog, and forget that a little of what you fancy does more good than masses of what you don't and that it is not the quantity but the food value that counts.

I reared my Dane puppy on five meals a day. The first when I got up in the morning consisted of a drink of Farex and milk, about two tablespoonfuls in half a pint of milk, later changing to cornflakes. Always feed a Dane off the floor especially when they get about three months old. I kept a stool for this purpose and the dog was always all her life fed on this. Danes' legs are too long to feed on the floor, they have to straddle the dish as does a foal eating grass and it does no good to their shoulders at all. My puppy at 11 a.m. had scraped raw 'leg of mutton cut' of beef or leg of beef. Later she did not like raw meat so I grilled it for two minutes a side, which she loved. The smell of grilled meat is very appetizing. The third meal was crumbled up slices of Hovis which must be stale. Sometimes I put slices into the oven for her to grind up or dipped this toasted bread into gravy from the grilled meat. The next meal was milk and cereal of some sort, either puppy meal soaked for at least an hour before feeding with boiling water, unsoaked puppy meal is very dangerous as it can swell in the puppy's tummy and cause acute indigestion; soaked in stock instead of boiling water it is very nourishing. I prefer brown bread at all times. Very occasionally I cooked (boiled) some liver and crumbled a little over her food which she wolfed, but beware of liver, it can cause diarrhoea, but it is an appetizer which few Danes can resist. This often tempts the owner to give too much, thinking she is giving the dog pleasure by giving it what it obviously likes. Over-indulgence is not good for Danes, as long as they have enough, and enough is five meals a day until about three months old. After that reduce the meals until at six months old it is having two meals a day consisting of $1\frac{1}{2}$ lb. of meat, one pint of milk a day and up to a small loaf of Hovis a day, plus the essential vitamins, calcium, minerals and trace elements which are vital if the dog is to not be rickety or suffer in growth or condition. Dane puppies have legs covered with lumps that do everything at first but grow straight later. Vets must be tired of people who bring their Dane puppies with enormous joints on the front legs imagining they may be starting rickets. These enormous joints are absolutely right for the size the dog will develop into. The legs grow straight as the puppy leaves puppyhood, and enormous bone is something to revel in and not be afraid of. So many Danes are too light boned and will never grow into large well-proportioned adults. You want to study top-class dogs, see the lovely let down of stifle on my Juno, choose a dog with a beautiful neck and head carriage. Juno was too thick in the neck really, but her wonderful bones earned her many prizes in the show ring and she was chosen to illustrates the German *Deutsche Dogge Handbuch* as the perfect Dane, instead of a German-bred dog. Many Danes seem to fail on hocks. They are either too wide apart or cowhocked. If too narrow behind this fault can be much improved when the dog is older by letting it have plenty of galloping exercise, chasing imaginary squirrels in woods is an excellent way of developing the inner thigh of a Dane which keeps the back legs wider apart, and counteracts the narrowness the dog may have been born with. Not only this, galloping strengthens the back. For the feet, trotting exercise is enough.

The feeding of Danes much depends on the sort of life your dog is to lead. My dogs were working dogs, they acted in films and television most of their lives and therefore spent long hours working. I never fed them whilst working as the nervous tension would have upset their digestion. Sometimes I was only called to the studio mid morning, so an early breakfast was possible, but if it was a very early call it was better to feed the dog in the lunch hour so she could have a sleep after the meal. The natural aftermath to a feed is a sleep and dogs don't work well when sleepy. If you are going into a show it is better to get up early and give the dog a good meal if you think your class will be late, but if you are going in the early part of the day don't give a meal, just keep a nice tasty morsel in your hand to make your dog look alert. I never did this myself, because my dogs were police-work trained, and to make my dogs look at their best in the show ring, I only had to show them some passing stranger and pretend that he was a criminal for the dog's head to be raised and the greatest possible look of interest on her face, ready for the command to 'get him'. I always stood at the end of the lead away from the dog so that the judge would have a clear view of her. I do not believe in perpetually placing dogs, holding their ears up, etc. If a dog is good you will win a prize, if not, the judge can't give the prize, although I have once proved beyond a doubt that a judge has given a prize to who was on the end of the lead, not what was on the end of the lead. This happened at a Dane show, my dog was unbeaten in all previous shows, and at this show someone absolutely inexperienced in showing dogs asked to take her in the first class. This she did and was put bottom of twenty-six entries. I was horrified, bitches with every fault were put above my bitch. I took her in the second class, she was immediately pulled into first place until the steward advised the judge of the previous placing. After the show the judge said to me: 'I made a bit of a mistake, didn't I?' This was very many years ago and I hope the same thing doesn't happen in modern times, it sickened me. That is why I prefer obedience, you can't feed your dog titbits and it really is a test of skill, devotion and training if you win. Once when I was working Juno in Test C in the days when food refusal was part of the test, the steward was testing Juno and she'd turned her head away four times on being offered food. The steward opened her mouth to put the food in and she held him until I told her to drop his arm. I was docked four marks for this. I consider she should have had four marks added for intelligence. What is the use of a dog that allows perhaps poisoned meat to be put in her mouth? I helped get the Kennel Club to drop food refusal after this as a useless and possibly dangerous performance. Dogs sent to boarding kennels were refusing food, having been trained only to take it from their owners.

It is vital in the home to teach your puppy to leave food on command. If he gets a bone in his mouth by mistake it could be fatal, so teach him to drop whatever is in his mouth on command, and to allow you to open his mouth and remove whatever is in it without a fuss or retaliation. Always if possible give another piece of food after he completes the giving up of the doubtful mouthful. Bones in food are particularly dangerous. Rabbit is an excellent food for Danes, but little bones can cause perforation of the gut and possible death, so if you give rabbit be sure to see there are no small bones left behind after you have taken out all the big ones. Chicken bones are also very dangerous as are mutton bones. The only bones a dog should have are big beef shin bones cut in half and the top cartilage taken away. The marrow is inclined to give a Dane diarrhoea so I always remove that. Except for teething and as playthings bones nowadays are not considered good for dogs and people who pressure-cook bones until they become a powder can cause severe constipation in dogs in the belief that they are giving calcium so essential to Danes for healthy growth. Calcium is best given in bone meal or proprietary additives.

Nobody can lay down the law on the amount of food to feed any puppy. It depends on its appetite, its size and what it needs to keep it growing but not letting it get too fat. It is a dangerous thing to let a Dane get too fat. Its legs are likely to bow; its tummy should look swollen after a good meal but should return to normal after about an hour.

Bloat is something every Dane owner dreads. Many valuable Danes have been put to bed at night well and healthy and been picked up dead in the morning from gas in the gut, the twisting of the gut kills them. Now in Germany there is a cure which stops this bloat; ask your vet if he keeps it. An emergency incision into the tummy to let the gas out has succeeded with one or two Danes, but few owners could do this. It is an emergency your vet will understand and race to your assistance should it occur. If your dog walks about and is fidgety, lying down and getting up, and the tummy looks swollen take it immediately to any vet. Small meals rather than large ones are less likely to cause bloat, but it seems to me this is caused by some malformation of the gut and is likely to happen to any dog at any time.

Water is essential at all times for dogs. Fresh clean cool drinking water left in an accessible place and changed twice a day helps the growth of the dog and keeps it fit. Excessive drinking should be treated with suspicion as in cases of diabetes dogs drink and drink and drink, but normally there should be no limitation to the amount of water a dog may drink. Do not in mistaken kindness, thinking it will help growth, leave milk around – a Dane should have a pint of milk a day and that is all; this can be dropped when the dog is adult. The first twelve months of growth in a Dane's life is vital to its long healthy existence, so feed it according to its condition and needs. Some Danes are finicky and will not put on weight, some have diarrhoea perpetually. If you meet this, take a sample of the dog's motion for analysis by a laboratory which will be arranged by your vet and ask for the *E. coli* count, especially, to be done, for an excess of this natural inhabitant of the gut can cause the dog to suffer with intermittent diarrhoea, hot ears, bloodshot eyes and lack of condition. Treatment with chloromycetin reduces these bacteria and the dog usually begins to thrive, but in doing this it also reduces the essential bacteria that should live in the gut and the dog should have vitamin B to counteract this and encourage the correct number of *E. coli* bacteria to return to the gut. Too much chloromycetin can be dangerous but this is something for your vet to decide. This excess of *E. coli* is sometimes got from the dam when the puppies are suckling. Kennels get infected and dogs from that kennel, however beautiful, never seem to thrive, they seem to suffer from a toxaemia which gives them headaches and excessively red insides to their ears.

If a dog won't eat I have found a home-made sponge puts on weight like nothing else. My Junia was persuaded to put on weight by this luxury food and ended up with a magnificent body when she was formerly a rather skinny youngster. Try to feed Danes at regular intervals. If travelling, take a meat meal with you which is easily fed on the journey. Tinned food is in most cases adequate meat food for Danes with, of course, variations in diet like coley fish, tripe, rabbit, chicken, etc.; the same food every day bores a dog as it does a human being. My dogs loved Yorkshire pudding. Vegetables are not necessary for Danes; they eat what grass they need, of which there are three separate varieties needed for perfect health. With modern re-seeding of pastures many of the grasses essential for a dog's health have been wiped out, so if you know of an old rubbishy patch of grass anywhere, take your Dane there sometimes and see if it doesn't wolf some of the coarsest and most uninviting types of grass. There are grasses for making a dog sick, grasses for helping bowel action, grasses for nourishment, and each one is known to your dog if allowed scope to eat it. Sometimes a dog or puppy will eat its own motions which revolts owners. This is the dog's way of trying to get the minerals and trace elements it needs. If all else fails I have known a dog's eating of horse manure to cure this habit. Dogs in the wild eat the gut of their prey and get what they need. Additives of proprietary manufacture should supply all a dog needs, but occasionally they don't. Then the dog seeks out what nature meant it to have and if no other dung is available it will eat its own in an attempt to rectify its deficiency. Never scold the dog. Take it to a vet who will test for a deficiency in some organ of the dog, but if all else fails remember horse dung. You may be revolted, but if you wash the dog's mouth and it recovers from its revolting habit of eating its excreta you will be grateful for this tip, it is only a temporary measure.

19

Early Training

The training of a Great Dane starts the moment it enters your home. It is very willing to come to you at that age because it has lost its mother, brothers and sisters and you are taking their place. All its life the command to come must be instantly obeyed. Danes are too big to be allowed freedom in public places without being obedient. It is useless saying to a squashed Poodle's owner that your dog only wanted to play. It is useless telling an old lady who has been knocked down and broken her thigh that your Dane never meant to bump into her legs, it was only chasing a sparrow. It is useless calling your dog to come back if your voice is so weak, and the respect that your dog has for you is so small, that practically any diversion is more exciting than you. So start young when you still have the respect and interest of a small puppy. Teach it to stay by voice and signal; if it gets up, don't think

'He's so tiny he's stayed long enough'. Be fair, make him stay only a few seconds at first, then rush back and love him and play. If he moves after the command to stay, return with a thunderous voice putting him back. Danes are far too sensible to get broken hearts by firm correction, they know which side of their bread is buttered and that butter comes from the owner's voice, the owner's pleasure and excitement at her dog being clever, and the joint games they have together after the *short* lesson. Keep the lesson short, one five-minute lesson twice a day is worth fifteen minutes of lengthy boring discipline.

Your puppy must tolerate his collar, a rounded stitched leather one, and then eventually a thick-linked choke chain I can let anyone have; it is not to my knowledge sold in shops. This type of choke chain is kind, will not hurt the dog or its fur if properly used, and in my opinion enhances the look of a Dane when it lies inactive on the shoulders of the dog in the show ring. I just can't imagine why people show dogs in nylon leads. I was one of the first to manufacture this type of lead over seventeen years ago or more and discarded them in favour of choke chains. Now they have become universal in the show ring and people string up their dogs so they can hardly breathe, forgetting the edges of the nylon leads are sharp. To me a Dane is a proud-looking aristocratic dog, it shouldn't need stringing up on a tight lead to make its neck arch, nor should it need its ears putting forward by being held in that position to show their carriage, for if a dog hasn't got good natural ear carriage it should be faulted on this point. If it is properly constructed by nature a Dane shouldn't have to be placed, it should be trained to stand in the way its owner wishes to show off its best points. I hate to see the tail of a Dane tucked between its legs at shows. This may only be because it is bored stiff with the tension at shows which is so easily communicated to a sensitive animal by its handler, but it looks bad.

Bill Siggers was always my favourite judge. If Bill gave your dog a first, or any prize, you knew you had a Dane worth owning from a beauty point of view. His knowledge came from a lifetime with Danes and included his winning Best in Show at Crufts and Champion Elch Edler of Oughborough, surely, the highest achievement anyone can attain. His kindness to beginners always gave them confidence and his willingness to tell you exactly what he thought of your Dane both good and bad must have helped many people to where they are in Danes. He liked handlers to let the dog show itself, for you couldn't fool Bill. When he was with Rank not only did he have a superb kennel of Danes but they were obedience trained too, and anyone who has seen a Dane working in obedience knows that in reality a Dane is a working dog, although obedience is far removed from being a Boarhound, the work the Dane originally did for its masters. Danes should always appear bold and ready to face anything; there is nothing so pathetic as a large animal like this showing fear at every shadow, looking around for ghosts at every sound, so I hope all breeders will concentrate on temperament, for in my training school in the last few years I have met dogs like this. I fear Danes becoming a popular breed and owners of single bitches breeding without really knowing what they are breeding from or to, reproducing dogs that do not do credit to the breed. A family bitch bred from is likely to get special care and attention and the puppies given a first-rate start in life, providing the owners understand a bitch's needs and the care and feeding of a litter.

Showing my Danes in the beauty classes never really appealed to me. My first Dane, Jean, must have been the ugliest Dane I'd ever owned but oh! what a wonderful character she had. I never noticed her much too long ears, to me she was perfect in every way. Jyntee was not a show dog but was one of the loveliest characters any Dane could be. Juno won forty-seven beauty prizes including one Best of Breed, and sixty-seven obedience tests, but her character was human, she never fluffed her part in any film or television she ever took part in, and was known at Pinewood as 'Take one Juno'. Both Juno and Junia were shown on a loose lead and a choke chain, Junia took four firsts in her first show and won some prize or other wherever I took her. Then I got fed up with showing, I didn't care whether my dog beat another dog on looks or conformation. I took a pride in seeing her on command wag her tail at the judge and look at the judge's face as if she was really pleased to see her or him. This is what I had trained her to do on the command 'talk' which training she was to use in all her films and television appearances. Nobody could ever tell that the person she was acting with was not her owner for she could put on love on command. I think all Dane owners could well copy this training with their dogs. A friendly dog on command is not an over friendly dog to all and sundry, it ignores everyone but its owner until told to do otherwise.

20

Early Management

I make no apology for reminding owners of Dane puppies what they must do when they get a new puppy or even an older dog, for memories are short even if you have had a Dane before.

Danes should have had their dew claws taken off by the breeder at an early age. Dew claws, except in breeds like Pyreneans which feature dew claws as part of the breed standard, are a menace and a danger to dogs, especially those that live in the country and may be allowed to gallop in the woods where the dew claws may easily get caught on a twig or something and literally nearly be torn off. I remember quite recently warning a lady to take her dog's dew claws off because of this danger, but she seemed to think it a bit cruel and put off having it done. The dog eventually tore its dew claw when out walking and had to have it removed after excessive bleeding which deeply worried its owner, and she rang me in great distress to know what to do. I told her to send it to the vet and have the torn one removed and also the other one as well. This she did but the dog suffered considerably as the plaster dressing was put on so tight the leg swelled. This should always be watched carefully, as some dogs even react to plaster allergically and a swollen leg can cause great pain and even disability. If it happens to swell, get the vet's attention quickly or even nick the plaster yourself to ease the swelling until the vet can be reached.

If you don't wish to remove dew claws for some unknown reason to me be sure to keep them well clipped with a guillotine obtainable from pet shops or Buck and Ryan, Tottenham Court Road, London WC1. This method of cutting nails is much kinder than clippers which pinch, and often cause the dog to fear this operation. Then it has to go to the beauty parlour or vet. Nail clipping should be a monthly operation carried out by a sympathetic owner. If this nail trimming is done regularly from the time the puppy is three months old or even earlier, the nails stay short. A Dane's feet look awful if the nails are allowed to grow too much. The quick will increase in length and the nails will be unable to be kept at a proper length if this is allowed to happen. Some breeders nowadays clip the new-born puppies' nails through the quick. This stops them ever growing too long, and although it sounds cruel, when the puppies are just born they feel very little. I've seen so many Danes' feet ruined by bad nail-cutting. I always trained my Danes on the word 'feeties' to lie on their backs, four feet in the air, to have their nails cut, as they were also trained to lie on their sides to have their teeth scaled by the vet, whereas many Danes have to have an anaesthetic to have this scaling done for them, they are so lacking in trust in their owners. These are regular beauty treatments and should not be left until the dog's nails are too long or the teeth all brown and smelly. A nice Dane is at all times wholesome to live with, but it can't be this on its own. Teach it from puppyhood to have its mouth opened and teeth gently rubbed with a piece of damp cotton wool.

If you intend trimming your dog's nails yourself it is quite easy to do if the dog stays still after proper training. You should be on the dog's right-hand side; lift each paw separately holding the paw just above the first joint. Get the guillotine knife on to the nail slanting the knife inwards, as the quick grows that way. You should be able to see the red quick if you do this operation with the light behind you. If you can't see it don't do it yourself, leave it to a more experienced person as once you've hurt and frightened the dog your chances of ever doing it kindly and safely are behind you. You can, of course, file the nails but this is a tedious and most uncomfortable experience for dog and owner. Danes' nails, especially if they have had road work which is so good for getting the feet nice and bunchy, become very hard. Only if constantly kept on concrete will dogs wear their nails down, so don't listen to anyone who says their nails can be kept in trim by about a mile of roadwork a day. I've never experienced this happening. If a nail is torn off in exercising the dog, the best thing to do is to get a wisp of cotton wool soaked in some antibiotic, wrap it round the nail and then wrap plaster over this. It usually stays on at least four or five days when the quick has healed. There is a good blood supply to the nails.

When Junia injured a toenail what I did do, which I regretted to the end of her life, was to take her into my bedroom at first to make sure she didn't bite the dressing off in the night. Then when I wanted to return her to her normal bed in my study she very nearly broke her heart thinking I was turning her away from me and for my sins she slept in my room until her end. I was the one who never really slept again, for a Dane, however quiet, breathes hard, turns over heavily, snores or grunts and if anyone is a light sleeper like I am, goodbye for ever to a peaceful night. I could not upset my dog. Her face was so pathetic and imploring when I tried to get her to sleep alone again, but then I am soft I know.

Medicines have to be taken at some time in a dog's life. Pills can, if necessary, be put in a lump of meat. As a trick teach your dog when young to catch things, she will then catch the lump on the command 'Dinner' and swallow it if she likes meat, without ever knowing there is a pill in it. I can hear my critics say, 'What about burglars throwing meat to a dog?' If your dog is not barking its head off and eager to pounce on any intruder I do not think she would need meat to make her amenable to burglars. I think she would go up and wag her tail and show them where the silver was anyway. I think it more important to have a healthy dog easily managed than to worry about burglars if I am properly insured.

Inoculations must, of course, be done when the puppy is about three months old, but some people forget the yearly boost dose; don't be one of those people. I have seen one brand of vaccine cause blindness in a dog. Be sure to ask your vet if he has known of this and not to use that particular brand. I find it essential to have inoculations in the flank rather than the shoulder.

Most Danes have peculiarities which every Dane owner recognizes. They all seem to love nibbling the owner's wrist and leading him or her around by grasping the wrist in their mouth, proudly arching their neck and walking him about willy-nilly. This is a delightful affectionate trait, but becomes painful as the dog gets big and powerful and the jaws so strong that the teeth are inclined to bruise the arm. Therefore I trained all my Danes to hold my arm with semi-open mouths, never to close. I did not want to deprive them of this 'love hold' but could not afford bruised wrists. Most Danes adore carrying things and the dumb-bell in obedience is not a trial to them. They have soft mouths and can carry eggs without breaking them. They make excellent gun dogs which most people don't realize. This fulfils their longing to work for the owner and the tenderness of their mouths is excellent for retrieving game. I taught Junia with pigeons because these are the nastiest things to retrieve, the feathers come off in the dog's mouth, but if they will retrieve pigeons other game is easy for them.

Danes jump well over fences; some have competed in trials where the high jump is in my opinion bad for Danes' shoulders, but seems to have been successfully overcome by Mrs Bensley and Mrs Dunkley, most successful trainers of Danes in competitive obedience. The long jump is perfectly harmless and great fun for dogs. They have excellent noses so scent discrimination is child's play for a Dane, and criminal work is heaven.

I believe in early training from eight weeks old in gun-fire; blowing up paper bags and bursting them accustoms the Dane to noise and makes thunder or gun-fire unfeared. Again all this must be done as one big game and much fun and laughter incorporated into the training.

Tracking should be started by hiding food, then articles and eventually human beings. Hide-and-seek in the house from an early age makes this training much appreciated by a Dane.

Do remember the younger you teach a dog new things, the easier for it to assimilate more and more each week. The training may start with you yourself going to a training session to see what criticism the trainer has of you. I believe any owner who comes to me gets the truth, the whole truth and nothing but the truth about herself, not always well received. This means she will be able, I hope, to train her dog not only to be obedient but to enjoy it. This enjoyment is what makes training fun. I've seen dogs' tails go down when they approach a training school. I've seen lively dogs hate every second of training; this is wrong. If your dog really hates obedience just take him far enough to be a good companion and go and buy a Border Collie who is trained by nature before you even have to start, and leave your Dane to be a naturally happy dog. However, in saying this I assure owners that Danes mostly enjoy training, and certainly it is highly necessary to reach a certain standard if the dog is to go everywhere with you and be an acceptable dog under all circumstances.

Danes are too big to be nasty tempered. They should be kind dogs unless the owner is threatened, when any dog worth its salt will protect its owner. If you don't get protected the dog doesn't truly love you. This, I fear, is the case with many dogs these days. They don't have enough human companionship to make the owner indispensable to their lives. Thus, the lovely bond I was lucky enough to have with all my Danes doesn't get developed and the owner is missing so much.

Doggerel A.B.C.

A is for all dogs however bad they be.
   I am absolutely certain they are not too bad for me.
   With firmness give correction, but give it lovingly.
   If you then obey instructions as to tone of voice
      you'll see,
   That the faults you thought were dog's faults, really
      lay with thee.

B is for biting dogs, good behaviour must be taught.
   For once they've bitten owner, or another dog
      they've fought,
   They are not safe for children, as they don't do
      what they ought.
   Sharp jerks upon the choke chain must be given
      when they're caught.
   Then down upon your knees you go, and their
      friendship must be sought.

C is for crafty dogs that will not come when called.
  Most owners think this dreadful, by their dogs they
    are appalled.
  On a cord you teach your dog to come in a safe
    place that is walled.
  With a five-yard cord you give a jerk, then his 'run
    away' is stalled.
  Thus quickly will he learn to come when his name
    is firmly bawled.

D is for dirty dogs who roll in a smelly spot.
  Don't beat them for it's nature, and just a doggy's
    lot.
  It's an ancient doggy custom to tell others what
    they've got.
  You must show the smelly spot to them, and tell
    them they 'must not'.
  They'll quickly learn what's right or wrong, or catch
    it pretty hot.

E is the easy way that owners hope to take.
  They think their dogs quite good will be without a
    jerk or shake.
  But they may find this lazy way trouble soon will
    make.
  And the dog may steal the Sunday joint, or the
    pretty birthday cake.
  It's better far to train them, then there will be no
    mistake.

F is for fear, that makes a dog seem quite insane.
  A nervous dog is pitiable, a worry and a strain.

But 'righteous fear' of doing wrong and causing
owner pain
Is good in dogs, and comes with training in the
main.
For by your voice, your smile, your praise, you
have to learn to train.

G is for a good dog, a dog we love to own.
A dog that does not grumble when his owner takes
his bone.
A dog that can be left to guard the home when
quite alone.
A dog who does not tear things up, or howl or
whine or moan.
A dog who calls his owner when she's wanted on
the phone.

H is for a happy dog who always wags his tail.
A dog who waits for master each evening without
fail.
A dog who does not fight dogs, even though they're
male.
A dog who comes to heel when told, and leaves a
rabbit's trail.
Sensible owners trained these dogs, and thereby
hangs a tale.

I is for the interest all dogs must learn to show,
When owner's busy training them, and teaching
them 'just how'.
But interest comes with quick commands, not a
voice that's dull or slow.

A romp and fun when training's done, and a hug
for your bow wow.
For it's up to you the owner to make the interest flow.

J is for all the joy that a dog feels when he's good.
The smile he gets when he knows he's done just
what he should.
The joy that his nose brings when he smells his
lovely food.
It's the joy of sweet peace when he's in a sleeping
mood.
It's the knowledge that he's worked just as well as
e'er he could.

K is for a kick that might cause injury,
Given often to strays who never should be free.
For kicks can do much harm that you do not always
see.
Dirty dogs get them, they should learn to use a tree.
Kind training is far better so train them carefully.

L is for love the most important thing of all.
If you don't love your dog you are no good at all.
For if a dog bites you or he won't come to call
His interest has flagged, and you've let his real love
pall.
To ensure a lasting friendship, you must your dog
enthrall.

M is for moping dogs who get chained up all day
Because they can't be trusted when their owner is
away.

They'll really have to learn when to work and when
　to play.
With the help of a choke chain you must teach
　them to obey,
For then they can be trusted to do just what you say.

N is for nasty dogs who chase the neighbour's cat.
　They must be firmly scolded and taught that 'that
　　is that'.
　They also eat linoleum or even Mother's hat.
　They kill the poor old chickens and chew up
　　brother's bat.
　A smack is what they need, not just 'oh dear' or
　　'drat'.

O is for the ordinary dog without pedigree or breed,
　He's just a pal, but just the dog some lonely people
　　need.
　He takes his walks alone, no chauffeur holds his
　　lead.
　He learns that life is good or bad without the help
　　of creed.
　He's faithful to the end when a saunter is his
　　speed.

P is for pedigree dogs whose training is for show.
　They travel to the big ones for master's in the
　　know.
　They learn to stand, to show their teeth, to run
　　quite fast or slow.
　To win first prize is great success, to lose is quite a
　　blow.

From training in obedience good manners soon will
flow.

Q is for queer dogs with long hair or sometimes none.
People like to have them for profit or for fun.
The little Mexican Hairless looks slightly under-
done.
The tiny little Min Pin with the great big cup he's
won
Looks lost beside the Great Dane basking in the
sun.

R is for rowdy dogs who will not stop that bark.
At first it may be just for fun and is treated as a lark.
But soon it is a nuisance all day and after dark,
And authority must step in and place its training
mark
On dogs that do not listen to their owner's firm
remark.

S is for sensible dogs who know when to obey.
When to run and when to come, and when to bite
in play.
For to be a happy dog you can't be good all day.
But you must know the tone of voice that makes an
owner say
'That's enough' then lie down and keep out of
owner's way.

T is for short-tailed dogs with hardly enough to wag
When they're roaming o'er the fields they need this
nature's flag,

For you can tell if it's up or down whether walks
    are fun or fag.
If game is being flushed it will stiffen or will sag.
Without this power to signal it's nothing but a tag.

U is for unpleasant dogs who puddle on the floors,
    Or bite the postman when he calls at other people's
      doors.
    And those with fleas who scratch themselves 'til
      they're a mass of sores.
    It's not the dog who is to blame for being in the
      wars.
    The owner should include her dog in all her daily
      chores.

V is the tone of voice that you and I must use,
    To teach our dogs when we mean to praise or to
      abuse.
    A warm soft welcoming voice is the one we want to
      choose,
    When calling dogs to come to heel, or one day we
      will lose
    Them, and they may chase sheep: then the owner
      we'll accuse.

W is for wicked dogs no training will they heed,
    On choke chain, or restraining jerks on a good stout
      leather lead,
    For they have learnt to live alone, no owner do they
      need.
    They get a shifty living as is the nature of their
      breed,

In other people's larders, or in dustbins do they feed.

X is for unwanted stray in heartbreak Battersea.
Countless eyes seek every day a home with you or me.
These unloved dogs are brought in here when strays or running free,
But can be bought and loved again for quite a tiny fee.
The joy when one is claimed is heartening to see.

Y is for your dog, quite the best of all.
Sometimes he's big and fat, sometimes he's thin and small.
Among the things you teach him is to bring his bone or ball
And not to fight or people bite, or the baby daughter maul.
And you must show your deepest love, when he comes to your call.

Z is not a dog, it's one that's lived its day.
It's now gone on to heaven, and this is what I pray,
That my loved dogs will meet me, if I ever get that way,
And once again they'll lick my hand, and with me ever stay.
For I believe that dogs have souls, they are not lifeless clay.

MORE ABOUT PENGUINS
AND PELICANS

For further information about books available from Penguins please write to Dept EP, Penguin Books Ltd, Harmondsworth, Middlesex UB7 0DA.

In the U.S.A.: For a complete list of books available from Penguins in the United States write to Dept CS, Penguin Books, 625 Madison Avenue, New York, New York 10022.

In Canada: For a complete list of books available from Penguins in Canada write to Penguin Books Canada Ltd, 2801 John Street, Markham, Ontario L3R 1B4.

In Australia: For a complete list of books available from Penguins in Australia write to the Marketing Department, Penguin Books Australia Ltd, P.O. Box 257, Ringwood, Victoria 3134.

In New Zealand: For a complete list of books available from Penguins in New Zealand write to the Marketing Department, Penguin Books (N.Z.) Ltd, P.O. Box 4019, Auckland 10.

'She has the comic genius of
Joyce Grenfell, the majesty of
Edith Evans, the eccentricity of
Margaret Rutherford and the
beguiling charm of Gielgud'
– *Daily Mail*

TALKING TO ANIMALS
'The Woodhouse Way'

Even before the first showing of 'The Woodhouse
Way', the *Evening News* was predicting that Barbara
Woodhouse's TV series would be more compulsive
than 'Crossroads' and more entertaining than
Morecambe and Wise. Sure enough, thousands
watched her, Giles put her in a cartoon, and she was
voted a TV personality of the year for 1980.

In this delightful autobiography Barbara Woodhouse again demonstrates that, whether it be in
horse-breaking, or book publishing, or the promotion of four-legged film stars, she always does things
the Woodhouse way.

'Like Mr [Clive] James, I'm a Woodhouse fan' –
Michael Parkinson

BENINGFIELD'S BUTTERFLIES

'A painter devoted to capturing the spirit of the countryside which endows his pictures with a quality that evades the mere illustrator' – *Guardian*

This edition features additional illustrations of Gordon Beningfield's beautiful stamp designs for the Post Office – an artist who has an 'extraordinary knack of combining the naturalist's eye for detail with the painter's feeling for patterns and textures' – *Sunday Times*

THE WORKS
Beryl Cook

'Beryl Cook is the nicest thing to happen to British painting for years . . . it makes me laugh out loud' – Edward Lucie-Smith

'Wildly funny and painted with the most loving detail . . . her way with bottoms, hands, bottles, newsprint and local vegetation is all her own' – Alan Ross

Introducing the world of Beryl Cook – Plymouth Argyle footballers, drag artists, transvestites, sailors on the Hoe, fish-and-chip shops, Teddy boys, fat barmaids, and all manner of wickedly funny goings on.

WEATHER FORECASTING
The Country Way
Robin Page

Observation of animal behaviour, plant growth or the wind, clouds, stars and moon is an ancient and well-tried method of weather forecasting. You may, for example, know what happens if it rains on St Swithin's Day or if there is a red sky at night, but what if it snows at Easter or if spiders spin long webs?

In this delightful book, Robin Page demonstrates that, by applying common sense to country lore, you need never have your holidays 'rained off' again!

TSI-TSA
a biography
George Mikes

You may wonder if a cat deserves a whole book devoted to him or her. You would be right to speculate; but Tsi-Tsa (her), black, beautiful and accomplished, is an exceptional feline. Tsi-Tsa is a vagabond. And her vagabonding causes George Mikes tears, terror and rueful exhaustion – and therein lies the nub of this book. Tsi-Tsa, one is happy to report, survives. She may not be aware of Chomsky, or understand the Balance of Payments, but her wisdom is now vast – *viva* Tsi-Tsa.

THE VIEW IN WINTER
Reflections on Old Age
Ronald Blythe

'Old age is not an emancipation from desire for most of us; that is a large part of its tragedy. The old want their professional status back or their looks . . . most of all they want to be wanted.' Ronald Blythe listened to all kinds of people who are in and around their eighties as they talked about their old age, to make this marvellous, haunting record of an experience that touches us all.

'Beautifully written . . . Moving but unsentimental and even oddly reassuring, it deserves, like *Akenfield*, to become a classic' – A. Alvarez in the *Observer*

LET'S PARLER FRANGLAIS
Miles Kington

Le Franglais est un doddle! Parlez Franglais, et le monde est votre oyster. Après 10 secondes, vous serez un expert, Belt Noir des languages – sans kidding. Ici Miles Kington présente 40 lessons hilarieux en des situations d'everyday. Dans le stately home, chez le dentiste, eyeball-à-eyeball avec la traffic warden, dans Soho après dark, toutes les phrases essentielles sont là. So, prenez un glass de bon plonk, light up une Gauloise et commencez l'aventure la plus exciting de votre existence!